LIVING CITIES

Report of the
Twentieth Century Fund
Task Force on Urban
Preservation Policies

LIVING CITIES

Background Paper
by
David Listokin

Priority Press Publications/New York/1985

The Twentieth Century Fund is an independent research foundation which undertakes policy studies of economic, political, and social institutions and issues. The Fund was founded in 1919 and endowed by Edward A. Filene.

BOARD OF TRUSTEES OF THE TWENTIETH CENTURY FUND

Morris B. Abram
H. Brandt Ayers
Peter A. A. Berle, *Chairman*
Jonathan B. Bingham, Emeritus
José A. Cabranes
Alexander M. Capron
Edward E. David, Jr.
Brewster C. Denny
Charles V. Hamilton
August Heckscher, Emeritus
Matina S. Horner
James A. Leach
Georges-Henri Martin
Lawrence K. Miller, Emeritus
P. Michael Pitfield
Don K. Price, Emeritus
Richard Ravitch
Arthur M. Schlesinger, Jr.
Albert Shanker
Harvey I. Sloane, M.D.
Theodore C. Sorensen
James Tobin
David B. Truman, Emeritus
Shirley Williams

M. J. Rossant, *Director*

Copyright © 1985 by the Twentieth Century Fund, Inc.
Manufactured in the United States of America.
ISBN: 0-87078-167-7

Foreword

It has been twenty years since the establishment of New York City's Landmarks Preservation Commission, and almost as long since the enactment of the National Historic Preservation Act. From those initial victories, what once was a largely elitist movement has taken on grass roots appeal. Mayoral candidates in many cities have found that it is good politics to promote preservation. National and local media have given widespread coverage to the aims of the preservationists, whether for the gentrification of run-down neighborhoods, campaigns for the protection of historic sites, or the transformation of old warehouses or buildings into impressive tourist attractions. Even developers, who once heedlessly bulldozed old buildings, now pay at least lip service to preservation.

How well has the preservation movement used its increasing power and influence? The Trustees and staff of the Twentieth Century Fund decided to appoint an independent Task Force to assess the record and determine where preservation has brought positive benefits and where it has not. The place of preservation as a tool of urban development seemed an appropriate focus for a group of authorities convened by the Fund, which has had a continuing interest in urban policy research. After all, legalized casino gambling had been touted as an effective tool for urban revitalization, until a Fund study of Atlantic City proved that while casinos have been profitable for their operators, they have added to the city's woes.

The Task Force, which was made up of an experienced group from across the country, concluded that preservation has on balance been a boon to development. In its view, preservation has not only brought an increase in jobs, both in the construction and service industries, but has also brought new life and vigor to many cities. Admittedly, preservation has not been without costs. It has meant the displacement of people who can least afford to be displaced. It has also thwarted or distorted some development projects. But by and large, the Task Force believes that preservation has helped, not harmed, new development.

Unquestionably, there is merit in preserving buildings of historic or aesthetic significance. Yet we ought to pay more heed than we do to the problems of the displaced—and we ought to be more discriminating than we are in making judgments about what is worth preserving. To be sure, many new developments are of mediocre design, whether modern—and dull—glass boxes or post-modern manifestations in overly ornate Beaux Arts style, but does that mean they should be forced to include the preservation of something representing what was mediocre at the turn of the century?

Perhaps the most useful of the many useful things done by the Task Force was its emphasis on the role of local government in land use policy, including, of course, preservation activity. With the federal role in preservation now shrinking, the cities must take a more active role in determining how best to use their limited resources in shaping and reshaping their physical environment. Leaving these matters to the cities will make for much more distinct differences in our cities than we have now.

As the Task Force points out, cities are quintessentially a mix of different industries, people, and styles, and the most vital of our cities are constantly changing, varying the mix in countless ways. What has distinguished the New World, and the United States in particular, from the Old is our openness, our dynamism, and our receptivity to change. It is all very well to celebrate the past, but we ought not be bound by it.

The Fund is grateful to the members of the Task Force and to David Listokin, who wrote the comprehensive background paper that accompanies the Report. We also give thanks to the following guest witnesses who appeared before the Task Force: Robert Peck, administrative assistant to Senator Daniel Moynihan; Jerry Rogers, associate director for Cultural Resources, The National Parks Service; Alexander Aldridge, attorney, Helm, Shapiro, Ayers, Anito and Aldrich; Rodney Little, director, Maryland Historical Trust; Truett Latimer, former State Historic Preservation officer, Texas; Kent Barwick, president of the Municipal Arts Society and former chairman, New York City Landmarks Commission; Edward S. Rutsch, president, Historic Conservation and Interpretation, Inc.; Norman Krumholz, former head of planning, Cleveland, Ohio; Richard Roddewig, consultant, Shlaes & Co.; and Bernard Frieden, professor of Urban Affairs, Massachusetts Institute of Technology.

The debates of the Task Force were lively, and its Report should encourage lively debate in all of our cities. That, in my view, would be a fitting tribute to its labors.

M. J. Rossant, DIRECTOR
The Twentieth Century Fund
June 1985

Contents

TASK FORCE MEMBERS

Orin Lehman, *chairman*
Commissioner, New York State Office of Parks, Recreation and Historic Preservation

Moon Landrieu, *vice-chairman*
Attorney, New Orleans; former Mayor of New Orleans

Richard Babcock
Retired Partner, Ross & Hardies, Chicago; professor of law, Duke University

Allan B. Jacobs
Professor of City and Regional Planning, University of California, Berkeley

Nellie L. Longsworth
President, Preservation Action, Washington, D.C.

Mary Means
President, American Institute of Architects Foundation, Washington, D.C.; former Vice President for Program Division, National Trust for Historic Preservation, Washington, D.C.

Martin Millspaugh
Executive Vice President, Enterprise Development Company, Columbia, Maryland; former Chairman and Chief Executive Officer, Charles Center-Inner Harbor Management, Inc., Baltimore

George Notter
President and Director of Design, Anderson, Notter and Finegold, Boston

Daniel Rose
President, Rose Associates, New York

John Rousakis
Mayor, Savannah, Georgia

Julien Studley
President, Julien Studley, Inc., New York

Richard Wade
Distinguished Professor of Urban History, Graduate Center, City University of New York

Robert F. Wagner, Sr.
Partner, Finley, Kumble, Wagner; former Mayor of New York City

Frederick C. Williamson
State Historic Preservation Officer, Department of Community Affairs, Providence, Rhode Island

John E. Zuccotti
Partner, Tufo & Zuccotti, New York

David Listokin, *rapporteur*
Professor, Center for Urban Policy Research, Rutgers University

Report of the Task Force

As citizens of the world's most dynamic nation, Americans have always looked toward the future. The fast-changing skylines of our major cities—New York and Chicago, Los Angeles and Houston—and, increasingly, our suburbs, clearly reflect our obsession with what is new. For most of our history, we have been fervent believers in progress, which has meant tearing down the old and building again, bigger and higher and bolder than before.

Yet we have recently become more mindful of our past. The heedless destruction in our cities that was an integral part of the nation's urban renewal efforts in the 1950s and 1960s led to the emergence of an urban preservation movement that had as its objective the conservation of the best of our past—historically, culturally, architecturally.

Advocates of preservation pointed out the costs, tangible and intangible, of demolishing existing buildings and wiping out entire neighborhoods in the name of progress and economic development. They were also able to demonstrate the benefits that derived from well-conceived urban restoration projects which served to revitalize run-down areas. Effective in winning legislation that provided incentives for restoration, the preservation movement enjoyed increasingly widespread popular support as exemplified most notably in our Bicentennial, that memorable celebration of our history as the world's oldest republic, its most enduring democracy.

The danger is that the pendulum could swing too far, that glorifying our past could result in hindering or even stultifying urban development, an essential ingredient for the economic vitality of our cities.

This Task Force, assembled to assess urban preservation and the role it plays in stimulating or retarding development in the nation's urban areas, does not believe that the historic preservation movement has gone to excess. To the contrary, we are impressed by the greater sensitivity to our past engendered by the preservationists and the economic stimulus that restoration projects have given to many of our cities. Accordingly, it is our considered view that the increasing awareness and appreciation of preservation activities have, by and large, served to promote, not impede urban development.

In our review and reassessment of the record of urban preservation, we were impressed with the private groups all across the United States that have been in the vanguard of the movement. Private preservation efforts spearheaded the transformation of what had been decaying historic areas into thriving showplaces attracting record numbers of visitors and fostering the creation of new businesses and new jobs in the process. These private organizations—there are now some 4,000—exercise a growing influence on architecture, land use, and urban planning. They have been instrumental in spurring an expanded role in preservation at all levels of government.

The federal government established the National Register of Historic Places to encourage the identification and protection of the nation's historic buildings; it currently offers a 25 percent investment tax credit for the rehabilitation of income-producing historic properties. At the state level, preservation offices, historic registers, and other programs designed to promote preservation are flourishing. And more than a thousand local government historic commissions have been set up; moreover, some local jurisdictions, along with some states, also offer tax incentives to preservation projects.

Inevitably, the growth in preservation activity has been accompanied by a growth in problems. The criteria for designating landmarks have not been as precise or as predictable as they should be, leading to abuses of one sort or another. Although preservation has been a significant force in revitalizing run-down urban areas, it has sometimes been used to delay or curtail desirable urban development. And there have been times when the accountability of preservation decisions has been open to question.

We concede that all too often current preservation and planning efforts go in opposite directions, creating confusion and causing conflict between preservationists, developers, and community groups in the nation's cities. Nor do we think that every old building with some pretension to architectural merit is worth preserving, or that landmarking should be a substitute for zoning. Time and again, the notion of giving landmarks designation to a building or a district comes under serious consideration in a city only after new development is proposed. This ad hoc, pressure-driven approach to preservation not only raises questions about the motives of preservationists; it also is detrimental to rational land use planning.

It need not be so. Preserving historic resources in urban areas has many virtues: it creates variety; it provides a sense of continuity; it affords access to air and light. But over and above these intrinsic values, preservation is an important tool for land use planning, especially in densely populated sections of our cities.

As we see it, preservation and development can and should be made to work together. Cities after all are most interesting and enjoyable when they combine the old and the new, the traditional and the avant-garde. They also are the most vital and livable when they offer diversity—high rises and church spires, crammed spaces and green spaces, streets of shops and streets of housing, of glass and steel, of cast iron and aluminum, of brick and timber.

What we have sought is a balanced approach, a strategy to protect our historical and cultural legacy while promoting the economic well-being of our cities. We recognize that it is not always possible to reconcile the interests of developers with those of preservationists, or the interests of property owners with those of the public at large. In such situations, we still think it possible to arrive at realistic and workable compromises. The Task Force, which itself is a mix of preservationists and developers, planners and politicians, is convinced that the best way to ensure that preservation and development work compatibly in our cities is by seeing to it that preservation activities are made an integral part of local urban planning.

Legitimating Preservation

Because our objective is vital and healthy cities, we do not regard preservation as an end in itself. New development is obviously essential, but so too is restoration. If we want cities that combine the new and the old, the bustling and the calm, the spare and the ornamental, then preservation must become a standard tool in the armory of urban planners, considered in the formulation of land use policy, not something that is treated either in isolation or as an afterthought.

Incorporating preservation into urban planning will not only make for better and more logical restoration and new development. It will also serve to strengthen the legitimacy of preservation. When local government designates a private building as a public landmark, it normally regulates and restricts the property rights of its owner. Such restrictions, challenged in New York City by the Penn Central Transportation Co., were upheld by the U.S. Supreme Court in 1978.* The majority opinion held that private property rights can be set aside if doing so serves a greater public good, which was the same rationale used in previous decisions affirming zoning regulation.

Still, the Court was careful to point out that overriding property rights cannot be done arbitrarily or capriciously. The assumption behind the ruling was that designation must be part of a "comprehensive plan," and that restrictions governing its use be reasonable. Unfortunately, these criteria are not always met. All too often local landmarking procedures are open to charges that they are neither reasonable in nature nor fairly applied, so that the law is vulnerable to fresh legal challenge. *Accordingly, this Task Force recommends that the identification and designation of historic buildings and sites be carried out in a manner that is careful, expeditious, and predictable.*

Setting Criteria

Defining adequate designation criteria is both a legal necessity and an opportunity for a community to delineate what it believes is important to its sense of history, heritage, and shared values. We encourage widespread participation by various community groups—including neighborhood schools, local historic societies, business or industrial organizations, and professional planning associations and architectural firms—so that scholarly interests are considered along with broader community interests.

Preservationists have long debated the wisdom of classifying and designating landmarks by some measure of historical significance. Those who favor such a system claim that grading historic resources will allow the most constructive use of limited resources—that is, to ensure that the most important properties are preserved. Opponents argue that grading will only add to existing difficulties in defining what is historically significant, inevitably condemning less important landmarks to benign

* *Penn Central Transportation Company v. New York City*, 438 U.S. 104 (1978).

neglect, and leading to a reversal of the idea that what deserves to be preserved includes edifices of state or purely local interest, not just national monuments.

What this Task Force considers essential is not the creation of a taxonomy of historic structures, but their protection. Whether or not historic landmarks are formally graded, a flexible, case-by-case review and negotiation of the extent of protection to be provided—in which the various interests, from property owners to developers to neighborhood groups, are represented—is needed.

Once the designation criteria are established, comprehensive surveys must be conducted to identify those historic buildings worthy of recognition and possible preservation. The comprehensive survey is both a means to an end and a useful exercise in its own right, but one that typically meets with (mostly routine) delays.

Timely and Predictable

The importance of acting on the surveys in timely fashion cannot be overemphasized. If a building has been identified as historically significant, it is essential that the designation process move forward promptly, predictably, and openly. Property owners must be notified, and a public hearing conducted, where the evidence for designation is put forward with a fair opportunity given for rebuttal. Then, a decision must be made, followed by an explanation as to why designation was or was not awarded.

To mitigate the negative effects of potential delays in official proceedings, landmarks commissions should make known their intentions. Properties under consideration for designation should be posted on a list of "eligible" structures, thus serving notice on affected property owners and potential buyers. *Once a building is listed as "eligible," we recommend that the landmarks commission arrange for monitoring the building to ensure that proper maintenance is continued and that no permit for demolition is granted.* Talk of designation has prompted irresponsible owners to desecrate or remove the very features that make a building worthy of preservation—for example, cornices, parapets, and iron work—or even to demolish the structure. If necessary, the landmarks commission should have the power to effect an interim designation for a specified period of, say, three to six months, during which the property owner would be required to meet maintenance standards.

The final step in the identification and designation of historic buildings, the completion stage, is critical if the process is to be comprehensive, timely, and predictable. Developers, who frequently have large loan commitments, need—and deserve—speed and predictability. In addition, completion entails educating landmark owners about the legacy in their care and informing them about how to deal with possible procedural requirements (i.e., how to apply for a rehabilitation review and permit) and how to meet maintenance standards. Speed is also critical for the formulation of appropriate land use policy.

While rapid completion of the survey-designation process is needed, there must be provision for reopening the process if buildings lose those qualities that made them eligible for preservation. Such reevaluations should be done on a periodic basis, say, every ten years.

The Public Role

The Task Force believes that an equitable, open, and thorough preservation policy requires extensive cooperation. What is required is joint participation by the private and public sectors—landmark owners, the development community, various levels of government, numerous private agencies—to protect our national heritage.

If our cities are to benefit from preservation, all levels of government must work together to foster preservation, leading by example, acting responsibly and responsively toward the historical inventory in their care. There must be competent administration of government preservation programs. Most important, there must be accountability. Public agencies that decide what—and how much—to preserve must be held accountable to some authoritative body in the first instance, and, ultimately, to the electoral process. As we see it, the federal preservation program should be held answerable to the Congress and the president; state programs to the state legislative body and the governor; local programs to the city or town council and the chief elected officials. Preservation decisions that overreach the legislated authority or, conversely, fall short of providing statutory protection should be subject to challenge.

The Federal Role

The Task Force affirms the federal government's special responsibility to the American national heritage. By law, government agencies must survey, inventory, and locate the historic resources owned or controlled by the federal government; any publicly or privately owned historic properties acquired, converted, or leased by government agencies must be used to the maximum extent feasible; when disposing of surplus landmark-quality properties, government agencies must favor users willing to preserve these structures. Since the way federal agencies carry out these responsibilities will influence the performance of state and local agencies, we urge that the heads of the federal agencies take the lead in seeing to it that the law is carried out.

We believe that the federal government must go further. It should actively encourage state and local preservation activity, serving as a clearinghouse for technical means of preservation; providing preservation literature; publicly praising successful preservation programs; and sponsoring conferences and other educational programs.

The Task Force urges the federal government to diligently carry out the specific responsibilities accorded it by the National Historic Preservation Act. One of the provisions of the act is the creation of a National Register of Historic Places as a means of documenting America's national heritage. National Register survey and designation activities are jointly financed by a matching grants system in which the National Historic Preservation Fund (NHPF) grants are matched by state governments. Even though the Reagan administration has not requested funding for the NHPF, Congress has voted it an approximate $25 million annual commitment. Nothing is served by this sparing act. The National Register survey and designation activities should be expedited, not prolonged. Hence, *the Task Force recommends that the federal government increase NHPF funding to finish the identification process by a certain date; the states must be equal parties in this endeavor, and must open their purses accordingly.*

Another provision of the National Historic Preservation Act covers the authorization of a review procedure (termed Section 106 reviews) designed to consider federal agency activity potentially harmful to structures listed or eligible for listing on the

National Register. It is important that Section 106 reviews proceed smoothly, protecting historic structures without impeding federal agencies from conducting their respective missions. State Historic Preservation officers and the Advisory Council for Historic Preservation should continue to work to streamline reviews. They should also adopt a rule of reasonableness in balancing competing public and private interests.

We also support continuation of the investment tax credit (ITC) for improving income-producing (residential or commercial) certified historic structures. Since the 25 percent ITC was passed in 1981, it has fostered a substantial amount of renovation. In fiscal 1984, for example, over 3,200 historical rehabilitation projects, valued at over $2.1 billion, qualified for the ITC. The 1984 report of the General Accounting Office to the Joint Congressional Committee on Taxation states that the tax loss to the Treasury was approximately five cents for every dollar of rehabilitation work generated. Thus, the federal government's costs for the ITC, in the form of forgone revenues, were small in comparison to the total amount spent on rehabilitation.

If the current Congress eliminates the ITC, it should create other federal incentives for preservation—equal to or greater than those reserved for new construction.* Such incentives should take into account the risks inherent in rehabilitating older structures with a depreciation or "life" expectancy less than that of new structures. A system of incentives, which can be accomplished either through the tax system or through outright appropriations, is essential to attract developers and investors to make use of older structures.

---

* *Ms. Longsworth dissents:* I object to incentives for rehabilitation that are only "equal to" those reserved for new construction. The result would be the demolition of older buildings and their replacement by new structures that take advantage of the full development potential of the space, creating the maximum income-producing building allowable under zoning. (While this may appear to be a more effective use of building sites, it encourages the destruction of important historic buildings, which directly conflicts with the rationale for enacting the rehabilitation tax credits.) If developers and investors are to consider rehabilitation of historic smaller buildings in areas where zoning permits greater height and volume, compensatory incentives are necessary, whether in the form of tax credits, accelerated building depreciation, or a shorter life.

Messrs. Lehman, Notter, Rose, Studley, Williamson, and Ms. Means join in this dissent.

The State Role

Two decades ago, in an effort to foster preservation the National Historic Preservation Act created a federal and state partnership whereby states were offered financial incentives to participate in the preservation of historic resources. *This Task Force believes that the time is long overdue for states to go beyond participation in the Section 106 process and to assume more direct responsibility for historic preservation.*

To begin with, some federal preservation measures could be carried out by the states. *We recommend, for example, that all states identify the historic resources within their borders on a state register of historic places.** States should be required to protect their historic resources from potentially harmful government action through their own Section 106-type reviews. We further recommend that preservation interests be integrated into state development and planning.

Perhaps the most critical state role in historic preservation in the future is the authorization of local government preservation activity; therefore, *the Task Force recommends that states continue to encourage local governments to engage in the full range of preservation activities*, by enacting new legislation such as the amendment to the state constitution approved in Texas to permit cities to use tax abatements to encourage preservation.

The Local Role

The Task Force believes that the primary arena for government preservation activity is at the local level. It is at the local level that the regulations governing the survival of a historic landmark are created and enforced. Local community participation is critical to the preservation process, and local communities are the clear beneficiaries of preservation. Thus, local government support for preservation should go beyond regulation to include creating a sense of pride in local history, perhaps best accomplished through the school system and civic celebrations. *This Task Force urges municipal governments to assume a new leadership role in preservation—to initiate programs and incen-*

---

* This is already done in a number of states (for example, California, Hawaii, Illinois, Kansas, and New York).

tives for preservation that are independent of, and go beyond, those available from federal and state governments.

The 1980 amendments to the National Historic Preservation Act provided for the "certification" of local governments in order to allow for a closer partnership among the federal, state, and local government officials concerned with historic preservation. Certification of local governments should proceed with all due speed.

The exact nature of local government preservation programs and incentives should, within the framework of prevailing federal and state preservation efforts, be tailored to local needs and interests. The following suggests the range of local government preservation measures that might be considered:

Building codes. Local building codes that require the use of new materials and modern construction techniques inappropriate to the rehabilitation of a historic property are antithetical to preservation; requirements for landmarks should be made flexible—provided that the proposed rehabilitation does not endanger health, safety, or welfare. In addition, municipalities should ensure that their building inspectors are made aware of, and will honor, special provisions for historic properties.

Loans and grants. Municipalities should provide financial assistance—in the form of grants, loans, or loan guarantees—for the rehabilitation and maintenance of landmarks. Funding could come from general taxes, intergovernmental aid, or such sources as the proceeds of bonds secured by the increase in property value in historic districts.

Property tax. Municipal governments should support historic preservation through local real estate tax policy. At a minimum, the local property tax should not penalize landmark owners. For example, if designation limits an existing landmark to its present use, the property should not be assessed at its "highest and best use."

Various property tax relief measures—such as a tax abatement for rehabilitation—also might be considered. These must be carefully screened because awarding property tax relief in an area such as the Northeast, where there are many historic properties, can disrupt tax collections, require additional work (for designating eligible properties) on the part of understaffed local historical commissions, and erode communitywide support if properties occupied by upper-income residents become eligible for tax relief.

If a property tax incentive is offered for historic preservation, it should be tied to a performance standard. A tax credit, for example, could be provided based on a percentage of approved restoration expenditures. But owners should not receive a tax incentive simply for owning a historic building.

Transfer of development rights (TDR). The Task Force endorses the transfer of development rights, which allows a landmark owner who might otherwise demolish his property in order to capitalize on its development potential to realize this gain by selling the development rights to the owner of an adjacent, or nearby, nonlandmark. At the same time, we recognize that application of this preservation strategy may play havoc with a city's zoning plans, which govern intensity of development. Transfers of development rights therefore must be examined in terms of overall zoning and land use considerations.

Hardship relief. In those cases where designation precludes the profitable use of private property, this Task Force believes that it is incumbent upon government to provide hardship relief. A definition of hardship must be clearly delineated (for example, a minimum rate of return on investment) and procedures for demonstrating hardship established. Once hardship is demonstrated under the specified conditions, the municipality should offer various relief options. These might include abatement of property taxes, finding a buyer for the property, or government purchase of the landmark. If these measures do not suffice or are not acted upon, withdrawal of the landmark designation should be considered. We consider hardship relief a necessary safety-valve mechanism that should be put into place.

Cushioning Displacement

Urban development projects have always involved the displacement of people. In the 1950s, bulldozers razed entire neighborhoods, uprooting whole communities. Now, inner-city neighborhoods are being revitalized in the form of restoration or preservation, helping to keep middle-class families in the cities and inducing new families to join them.

But if gentrification has helped to revive and restore crumbling neighborhoods and has improved the quality of life for all who reside in them, it also has entailed displacement, usually on a smaller scale than the mass exoduses of a generation ago. This is no solace to those who are displaced, typically the old, the poor, and minorities. They are the people, of course, who are least able to bear displacement. Clearly, there is a need to devise preservation policies that minimize the burden on the poor. It is not merely a question of money. Preservationists above all should be sensitive to the psychological jar of displacement and take steps to cushion it.

Private Responsibilities

Private citizens and groups were the pioneers of the preservation movement. They initiated the identification and protection of natural and historic resources, and have lobbied long and effectively for government recognition and assistance. Their efforts have been successful beyond their most optimistic expectations. Government has been enrolled in the preservation movement, and thousands of private groups at the grassroots are doing what they can to preserve sites and buildings. Thus, preservation is no longer looked upon as an exercise in elitism. Our national heritage is widely regarded as the concern of all citizens and of all levels of government.

Given the progress that has been achieved, it would be understandable if at this stage preservationists everywhere rested on their laurels. They have in a real sense achieved victory. But much is still to be done by private-sector preservationists. *This Task Force calls upon preservationists everywhere to step up their efforts at the same time that they guard against the excesses of those who would sacrifice development on the altar of preservation.* To be blunt, a mature and responsible preservation movement must take pains to police itself.

The private preservation movement must increase its efforts to strengthen and expand its partnership with institutions in the public sector that are engaged in preservation activities. We recommend the following measures:

Advocacy. At this period of financial stringency at the federal level, private organizations must form coalitions and become even more persuasive if they are to obtain greater financial commitments for historic preservation from state and local governments.

Public relations and communications. Private organizations should work to improve public awareness of the benefits of preservation for the nation's cities.

Information and technical assistance. Private organizations should aid in the dissemination of information about preservation methods and techniques as a means of enhancing the quality of preservation measures.

Financial participation. Private organizations should push for wider adoption of revolving funds for preservation and for preferential treatment from local lending institutions, which have become especially critical in light of diminishing federal loan and grant subsidies for rehabilitation of historic properties.

Easements. Private organizations should accept and monitor donated easements. The easement donation has the advantage of being flexible and allows the donor a federal tax write-off. But the application of easements as a preservation strategy can be realized only if there are entities to accept and monitor them. Private preservation organizations can and should act in this capacity.

Other support. Private organizations can lend support in other innovative ways. For example, they can "adopt" a landmark building by paying for maintenance and visitor-related services (i.e., brochures and guides). Such a role has been assumed by Cooperating Associations, which work to protect and make available to the public the historic and natural resources under the auspices of the National Park Service. Other private organizations might consider their example.

This Task Force believes that there are some groups in the private sector who have a particular responsibility in regard to historic preservation. These include the National Trust for Historic Preservation, professional architectural institutions, and the community of American historians.

As the only national, private preservation organization chartered by Congress, the National Trust for Historic Preservation has a unique role and a responsibility to guide and support the loose network of state and local preservation organizations. *The Task Force urges the National Trust to strengthen its efforts to disseminate information to policymakers and those whose investment choices influence the future of historic structures; to communicate to audiences outside the preservation community; to manage its own historic properties wisely so that they serve as a model for wide emulation; and to bring balanced leadership in an area prone to conflict.*

We believe that schools of design and architecture are seriously negligent in the area of historic preservation, ignoring the benefits of adaptive reuse of older buildings and the potential for successful integration of existing structures and new construction. *This Task Force challenges schools of design and architecture, as well as professional architectural societies such as the American Institute of Architects, the American Planning Association, and the American Society of Landscape Architects, to place greater emphasis on preservation concerns in educating practitioners of design and planning.*

The involvement of professional historians in preservation has primarily been in a technical capacity—as consultants, as members of boards, and as advisers to public officials. We believe that it is now time for historians to join with the practitioners of the historic preservation movement. *We urge the major national associations of professional historians to give attention to preservation in their regional and national conferences, to include preservation in their job placement and counseling services, to maintain lists of members willing to consult with local preservation committees, and to routinely list meetings on historic preservation along with notices about other conferences.* We also urge teachers of American history to incorporate preservation into their regular curriculum, especially at the primary and secondary school level.

Preservation in the Future

The preservation movement has come a long way. There is now little argument over the need to preserve what is left of our national, regional, and local heritage. They are not mere museum artifacts, but a living part of our civilization. It might appear that a nation of immigrants, composed of many ethnic stocks, has no special interest in the tangible remains of the nation's past. Yet those who have come from different lands seek—and treasure even more than some native citizens—common roots and continuity. The preservation movement is playing an inestimable role in making Americans of all of us.

Preservation, though, is not solely concerned with the past. It has prospered as a movement because of its emphasis on living communities, particularly urban communities. It has taught that preservation offers more opportunities than barriers, and that wholesale destruction of the old can be detrimental to the new.

Developers have come to appreciate the investment potential of our older existing building stock just as preservationists have come to realize that the best way to protect what is old is through judicious merger with the new. Where individual buildings and entire districts have been designated in timely manner and where developers have been alerted to the need for preservation at an early stage, projects have been aesthetically enhanced, project sponsors have profited, and community residents have enjoyed lasting benefits.

There are, of course, exceptions. But those exceptions are becoming fewer. In most cases they are caused by the neglect or flouting of established procedures, not by faulty procedures, or by a lack of recognition of significant historic structures until the wrecker's ball is about to strike, or by a failure of one or another interest to recognize the validity of other interests.

The principal concern of this Task Force is to ensure that our cities become better places in which to live. Preservation has been making that happen. Our recommendations are put forward in the hope that they will guide future public and private preservation efforts to keep our heritage intact while stimulating urban development. We need to do both if we are to serve this generation of Americans and generations to come.

Background Paper

by David Listokin

Preface

For a long time, a majority of Americans shared Jefferson's view that cities were "pestilential to the morals, health, and liberties of man"—yet by 1920 the majority of the population lived in areas classified as urban. While this trend toward urbanization has continued, the central city core has increasingly been buffeted by economic and social malaise. For the past half century, government intervened to bolster the sagging fortunes of America's cities—with varying levels of success. Over the past two decades, the historic preservation movement—a joint private and public effort—has become an effective force for urban revitalization. The time, however, has clearly come for the preservation movement to be examined; I would like to thank The Twentieth Century Fund for giving me the opportunity to do so.

The background paper was written to assist the deliberations of the Fund's distinguished Task Force on Urban Preservation Policies. It traces the evolution of the historic preservation movement, describes its current application, and invites reconsideration of the status quo. The latter is most important, for while historic preservation has achieved much in a short time, and many existing strategies are working well, complacency is a danger.

The background paper draws upon both the preservation literature and interviews with preservation practitioners and critics. At the risk of slighting other works of great merit, the following must be cited as providing invaluable background: *With Heritage So Rich* (United States Conference of Mayors), *Presence of the Past—A History of the Preservation Movement in the United States Before Williamsburg* (Charles B. Hosmer), and *A Handbook on Historic Preservation Law* (Christopher J. Duerksen). The Advisory Council on Historic Preservation, the National Park Service, and local preservation commissions in 160 cities described in interviews their accomplishments and future challenges.

The author also extends his appreciation for the many helpful comments on the background paper given by the Task Force members and its chairman, Orin Lehman, and for the assistance and perspective provided by Frank B. Gilbert of the National Trust for Historic Preservation.

Research assistance was provided by many individuals. James J. Nemeth supervised the telephone survey of local preservation commissions. The manuscript was edited and reviewed by Judith Hancock and Arlene Pashman. Typing was handled by Lydia Lombardi.

The author acknowledges the debt of assistance provided by so many; errors are his alone.

Introduction

Writing more than a century ago, de Tocqueville remarked that democratic nations "prefer the useful to the beautiful and require that the beautiful should also be useful." This sentiment helps to explain why, in the past, American society paid little heed to its historic environment. Successive waves of new building technologies, materials, and space needs fostered the demolition of much of what was constructed in preceding generations. The fate of buildings listed in the Historic American Building Survey is illustrative; a significant share of the entries on the roster, ranging from the Chicago Stock Exchange to Penn Central Terminal, has been destroyed.

Indifference to the past characterizes America's history. In part, that is a source of strength—a focus on the future, an appetite for the new, and a refusal to be mired in the past. The American detachment from, if not oblivion to, the existing built environment is also perceived as a serious societal flaw. The lack of preservation sentiment, resulting in wholesale demolition, was criticized in an 1871 *Harper's Weekly* cartoon (Exhibit 1) depicting late-nineteenth-century American society marching callously on while the physical legacy of the eighteenth century is being destroyed. (Interestingly, these nineteenth-century row houses, Second Empire buildings, and other replacements are among the housing treasured today by preservationists.) A century later, a cartoon in a 1969 *New Yorker* (Exhibit 2) conveyed the same message—America disposes of its past.

But increasingly, Americans are beginning to view their historical environment as being as "beautiful" and as "useful" as new construction. In the mid-1950s, about twenty cities enacted ordinances encouraging or requiring preservation; by the mid-1960s, there was a fivefold increase in the number of

Exhibit 1

The March of Modern Improvement

Harper's Weekly, October 28, 1871; drawn by C. S. Reinhart.

such ordinances. By the time of the nation's bicentennial in 1976, five hundred cities had passed preservation laws; today, nearly one thousand local governments and every state have preservation laws on the books. Entries on the National (federal) Register of Historic Places mushroomed from roughly 2,000 in 1970 to an estimated 37,000 as of April 1985.

Historic preservation, once solely an urban phenomenon, is now manifest in all areas of the country—preservation commissions, designation controls, and similar appurtenances now exist not only in the cities but also in suburban and rural locations. Support for historic preservation has come from all levels of government, often in the form of landmark and historic area designations, rehabilitation tax incentives, and the like. The acceptance by the courts of these multifaceted instruments has assured preservation's acceptance. Public interest and involvement in historic preservation have grown tremendously. Once a passion that stirred only the experts, historic preservation now attracts the layman. Designation meetings can now bring out the neighborhood community as only major zoning-change meetings did in the past. Preservation's entry into the social mainstream has been exploited by numerous developers opting to embark on rehabilitation projects, albeit other builders view preservation as a deterrent to new construction.

In the flush of the new embrace of historic preservation, difficult issues remain to be addressed: What have been the impacts of historic preservation? What benefits have been realized? At what cost (social and economic) and at whose expense? How can preservation's benefits be enhanced and its adverse consequences mitigated? Should preservation activities continue to be publicly regulated and supported as they have in the past? Is historic preservation truly in the public interest?

In light of the proliferation of historic preservation efforts, it is essential that these critical issues be examined, so that the growing preservation momentum will be sustained for the welfare of the public. This background paper considers how resources noteworthy from a historic, architectural, and/or cultural perspective are—and should be—preserved. The discussion focuses on the preservation of the built environment in metropolitan areas.

Drawing by Saxon; © 1969
The New Yorker Magazine, Inc.

"I feel I should warn you. They've taken down most of Boston and they're putting up something else."

Exhibit 2

— 1 —

Background and Evolution

The phrase "historic preservation" is so elastic that any sort of project can be justified—or any change vilified—in its name. In a sense, every event is "history. . . ." Art and architectural historians, especially important to preservation, are equally flexible in their views of "historic significance," as shown by their recent interest in the art deco Coca-Cola signs, quonset hut offices, and White Tower diners that once horrified historic preservationists.

— Carol M. Rose[1]

Like Rip van Winkle, Americans wake up to find the anchors of their memories gone; they can't go home again because home is now a Dairy Whiz doing business in the middle of a sea of asphalt, and after the fad for Dairy Whiz fizzles, it too is replaced. . . . How can people learn to appreciate what they've already destroyed? This litany of dire results is the logical end of a failure to practice preservation.

— Tony P. Wren and Elizabeth B. Mulloy[2]

Historic preservation is as old as ancient history. The Romans, for example, saw preservation as a means to "rekindle interest in ancient patriotic virtues."[3] Gibbon describes the preservation efforts of the Emperor Majorian in 453 A.D. in *The Decline and Fall of the Roman Empire:*

> The monuments of consular or imperial greatness were no longer revered as to the immortal glory of the Capitol. . . . They were only esteemed as an exhaustible mine of materials, cheaper and more convenient than the distant quarry. . . . Majorian, who had often sighed over the desolation of the City, applied severe remedy to the growing evil. He reserved to the Senate the sole cognizance of the extreme cases which might justify the destruction of an ancient edifice; imposed a fine of 50 pounds of gold on every magistrate who should presume to grant such illegal and scandalous license; and threatened to chastise the criminal obedience of their subordinate officers by a severe whipping and amputation of both their hands.[4]

Skipping more than a millenium to the beginning of modern preservation efforts in Europe in the nineteenth century, major European powers institutionalized—through protective laws and societies—the preservation of nationally significant historic buildings and sites. In the 1830s, King Louis Philippe of France promulgated laws to ensure the "endurance" of historic buildings.[5] Further protections followed: In 1906, French law extended protection to places of beauty; in 1930, the French Parliament enacted the "Law With Regard to Historic Monuments" providing for the "classification" of notable private buildings, which protected such structures from demolition.

France was not unique. Other European nations attempted to preserve their heritage. In England, a Society for the Protection of Ancient Buildings—a private organization—was founded in 1877. A generation later, in the early twentieth century, the English Parliament provided for public control of the nation's historical legacy through the passage of the Ancient Monuments Consolidation and Amendments Act. Similar private preservation organizations and protective laws came into being in Germany, Switzerland, Austria, and other European countries throughout the late nineteenth and early twentieth centuries.

By contrast, historic preservation was a much later development in the United States. While some preservation sentiment can be traced back to the founding of the nation, this is the exception rather than the rule. In the vigor of its growth, America preferred the new and had little reverence for the products of prior generations. Sentiment and consensus for preservation did not coalesce until midway through the twentieth century. America was a reluctant and late convert to preservation; yet, the recent embrace is growing in strength and scope.

The Origins of Historic Preservation in the United States

Until the late nineteenth century, there was little by way of physical structures in the United States that was not fair game for destruction.[6] Still, voices began to be raised against the demolition of buildings identified with the nation's history. During the early 1800s, for example, a protest arose at the impending demolition of the "Old Brick" Meeting House in Boston—a site of significance during the Revolutionary War. But these protests were to no avail, and "Old Brick" was demolished in 1808, joining many other historical properties.

Protesters were successful in 1816, however, when the old State House in Philadelphia, where the Declaration of Independence had been signed and the Constitution written—now known as Independence Hall—was put up for sale for building lots. As a result of the protests, the city of Philadelphia purchased the hall for $70,000. Shortly thereafter, Philadelphians restored it and replaced paneling that had been removed and sold a few years earlier. Another successful early preservation effort was the New York state legislature's decision, in 1850, to provide funds to save George Washington's headquarters in Newburgh, New York.[7] But not all state legislatures were as generous, as the fight to save Mount Vernon makes clear.

George Washington, often referred to as the Father of Our Country, is in many respects the father of historic preservation in the United States.[8] In the mid-1800s, there were few figures as revered; yet this did not deter a group of businessmen from seeking to purchase Mount Vernon, demolish the structure, and use the plantation for a hotel site. The news did not provoke official action. The state of Virginia would not appropriate the funds to purchase the property in order to save it; it did, however, charter the Mount Vernon Ladies' Association of the Union, a private organization seeking to protect Mount Vernon from demolition.

It took a remarkably dedicated woman—Ann Pamela Cunningham—to preserve Mount Vernon. In December 1853, she wrote an article for the *Charleston Mercury* pointing to the debt that all Americans owed Washington: "Can you be still with closed souls and purses, while the world cries 'Shame upon America' and suffer Mount Vernon, with all its sacred associations, to become, as is spoken of and probable, the seat of manufacturers and manufactories? . . . Never! Forbid it!"[9]

Over the next decades she negotiated with Washington's heirs to delay the sale of Mount Vernon to commercial interests and founded ladies' associations throughout the country to collect needed monies. She also enlisted the support of a noted orator, Edward Everett of Massachusetts, who delivered 139 appeals for Mount Vernon's preservation, averaging almost $500 for each appearance.[10] Through these combined efforts, Cunningham succeeded in raising $200,000—a princely sum for the time—to purchase and ultimately restore Mount Vernon.

The saving of Mount Vernon inspired other efforts at protecting and preserving sites of historic value. In 1856, the Hermitage (Andrew Jackson's home near Nashville, Tennessee) was purchased by the Ladies' Hermitage Association—modeled after the ladies' associations formed by Cunningham. In 1876, the Old South Meeting House, in Boston, Massachusetts, was rescued from demolition.[11] Other structures saved in the late 1800s included Washington's headquarters in Morristown, the encampment at Valley Forge, and Hamilton Grange, once the home of Alexander Hamilton.

A number of pioneering preservation organizations and societies were established. In 1888, the Association for the Preservation of Virginia Antiquities was formed to protect Jamestown, among other sites. Patriotic societies, such as the Daughters of the American Revolution and the National Society of the Colonial Dames of America, began to include preservation in their agendas. There were also some nascent attempts at bringing government, or at least public figures, into preservation activities. A notable example was the chartering of the Memorial Association of the District of Columbia in 1892.[12] But the thrust of preservation activities was still decidedly private. Government involvement was limited to chartering preservation groups. It would be many years to come before there was more active government intervention.

The definition of "historic" in this early period was the physical legacy of great moments of history—particularly if they imbued a patriotic response on the part of the observer. When it considered state purchase of Hasbrouck House, George Washington's headquarters in Newburgh, New York, the New York State Legislative Committee reported:

> No traveller who touches upon the shores of Orange County will hesitate to make a pilgrimage to this beautiful spot, associated as it is with so many delightful reminiscences with our early history, and if he have an American heart in his bosom, he will feel himself a better man; his patriotism will kindle with deeper emotion; his aspirations of his country's good will, will ascend from a more devout mind for having visited the "headquarters of Washington."[13]

In most cases, the individual building or site rescued from demolition was then operated as a museum or the equivalent. Independence Hall, Mount Vernon, the Hermitage, and the Hamilton Grange were all saved in this fashion. The concepts of preserving an entire neighborhood or of lived-in historic structures—thus conserving the area-wide ambience of everyday life—had not yet been conceived. And while preservationists could number their successes in scores of buildings rescued, thousands of historic structures—some of major call upon the nation's history and conscience—were destroyed.

The Next Stage

Starting in the late nineteenth century, preservation efforts took on a new vigor. The Society for the Preservation of New England Antiquities, for example, incorporated in 1910, saved many buildings of note throughout New England. In contrast to the early period, when preservation was oriented solely to the historic and patriotic, the beautiful was now included. Thus, when William Sumner Appleton stated the purpose for organizing the Society for the Preservation of New England Antiquities, he said it was "to save for future generations structures . . . which are architecturally beautiful or unique, or have special historical significance. Such buildings, once destroyed, can never be replaced."[14]

There was also a growing sensitivity to the larger area setting, to the neighborhood and vista, as exemplified by John D. Rockefeller's restoration of colonial Williamsburg in the mid-1920s.[15] The Williamsburg approach inspired Henry Ford to establish Greenfield Village in Dearborn, Michigan, in 1929. Greenfield consisted of over one hundred reconstructed and restored seventeenth-, eighteenth-, and nineteenth-century buildings laid out in a town setting so as to convey the mood and collective architectural vista of the past.[16] Other village restorations followed, such as Old Sturbridge Village in Massachusetts, Schoenbrunn Village in Ohio, and James Fort in Virginia. In their time, Williamsburg and progeny were at the leading edge of preservation. Still, while these village re-creations went one step beyond the preservation of individual buildings, and while they conveyed the ambience of yesteryear, they were nonetheless artificial creations and museums as opposed to "living" entities. There was some limited "living" preservation, as a few neighborhoods such as Vieux Carré in New Orleans were designated historic enclaves, but this was very much the exception.

Government also cautiously intervened in historical preservation. The federal government's involvement was stirred by a threatened defacement of the Civil War battlefield at Gettysburg, Pennsylvania, in the late 1800s. Congress appropriated funds for its purchase and authorized the secretary of war to condemn the site.[17] Other Civil War purchases soon followed. The first encompassing federal legislation was the Antiquities Act of 1906 (Public Law 59-209), which authorized the president to designate as national monuments those areas of the public domain containing historic landmarks, historic and prehistoric structures, and objects of historic or scientific interest.[18] The designation was limited, however, to properties and sites of significance to the nation as a whole and to sites on land owned or controlled by the federal government. A decade later, the National Park Service (NPS) was created to protect historical and national parks. The NPS was to play a major role in historic preservation in the United States.

Both the Antiquities Act and the NPS were restricted to the designation and care of historical resources under the federal domain. But in 1935, when President Franklin D. Roosevelt signed the Historic Sites Act into law, federal participation in historic preservation broadened. The legislation set forth a ringing call for preservation: "It is declared that it is a national policy to preserve for public use historic sites, buildings, and objects of national significance for the inspiration and benefit of the people of the United States."[19] The act also empowered the NPS to inventory the nation's most significant historic resources, both those in private as well as public hands. This charge was realized by the National Survey of Historic Sites and Buildings, started in 1937, which inspired further cataloging by the Historic American Building Survey and the Historic American Engineering Record. These NPS surveys laid the groundwork for cataloging and documenting the nation's historic resources. In the 1930s, the NPS also assumed a caretaker role for significant historic sites. In this decade, Ford's Theatre, Fort McHenry, the Morristown encampment, and Fort Laramie were declared national historic sites or monuments.[20]

The growing government involvement in preservation was not limited to federal intervention. Local governments also entered the picture. Starting in the 1920s municipalities began to enact preservation laws authorizing the designation and protection of local historic buildings and neighborhoods. Historic district designation, which either prohibited or, at least, delayed or discouraged inappropriate alterations or demolition, was adopted in New Orleans (1925, 1937), Charleston (1931), San Antonio (1939), and numerous other communities.

States also began to support preservation efforts on a limited level. State involvement included establishing road markers and plaques calling attention to the presence and significance of historic resources; applying eminent domain powers to acquire sites of historic significance; providing limited financial assistance (ranging from property tax exemptions to start-up funds) to historical societies; and enacting enabling legislation authorizing municipal preservation controls. While the range of state preservation activity was broad, with the exception of enabling local government to conduct preservation activities, it was neither vigorous nor particularly significant.

Professional group interest in historic preservation also grew. In 1940, the Society of Architectural Historians and the American Association for State and Local History were founded. In 1947, the National Council for Historic Sites and Buildings, the predecessor of the National Trust for Historic Preservation, was organized. Two years later, Congress chartered the National Trust for Historic Preservation to foster preservation awareness and advocacy.

But at the same time that these preservation activities got under way, there was a massive loss of historic resources. Government urban renewal programs and the construction of the interstate highway system resulted in wholesale destruction of many significant buildings and areas in the 1950s and 1960s. The loss was so great as to spark increased government intervention to protect the historic stock.

Preservation Comes of Age

Federal enactment of the landmark 1966 National Historic Preservation Act served as a major catalyst for the expansion of preservation activity. The act declared that "the historical and cultural foundations of the nation should be preserved" and established four means to achieve this goal: the National Register of Historic Places to inventory the nation's cultural resources; a National Historic Preservation Fund to provide financial aid (the Fund was formally established in 1976); a new executive-level body, the Advisory Council on Historic Preservation (ACHP), to advise the president and federal agencies on preservation efforts; and a review process, Section 106, spearheaded by ACHP, to evaluate federal actions affecting National Register properties.

Other federal legislation soon followed. In 1969, the National Environmental Policy Act required that environmental impact statements document the effect of federal activity on historic resources, with consideration given to means to mitigate adverse consequences. Financial aid, in the form of federal tax incentives, was offered—first by the Tax Reform Act of 1976 and then, more extensively, by the Economic Recovery Tax Act of 1981.

Inspired by this series of supportive federal legislation, preservation became a growing national phenomenon. (See Table 1.) In 1968, a total of 1,204 properties and districts were listed on the National Register of Historic Places. By 1970, the entries had practically doubled at 2,395; two years later, the entries again doubled, reaching almost 5,000—a spiraling matched in 1975 when the number of entries topped 11,000. The National Register continued to grow, reaching an estimated 37,000 entries—containing an estimated total of 200,000 buildings (about 0.25 percent of the nation's building stock)—as of 1985.[21]

Other data reflect the growing momentum. In 1968, the Advisory Council on Historic Preservation reviewed five cases under the Section 106 process; by 1981, the annual volume had climbed to 2,700 cases. Federal grants-in-aid for preservation activities mushroomed from a modest sum of $500,000 in 1968 to over $50 million by the late 1970s—though it has been cut back by the Reagan administration.

Federal financial support for preservation in the form of tax benefits has played a particularly significant role in spurring the enormous growth in preservation activities. Following enactment of the Tax Reform Act of 1976, approximately 500 rehabilitation projects, representing an investment of roughly $140 million in renovation expenditures, qualified for favorable tax treatment. By 1981, these figures increased to almost 1,400 projects representing an investment of approximately $750 million. The pace of investment accelerated still further following the authorization of investment tax credits (ITCs) provided by the Economic Recovery Tax Act of 1981. In 1982, 1,800 preservation projects, encompassing a rehabilitation expenditure of $1.128 billion, were approved for ITC purposes. The number mushroomed to 2,600 projects, representing an investment of $2.165 billion, in 1983; 3,200 projects with a $2.123 billion rehabilitation investment qualified in 1984; and 3,600 projects with a $2.400 billion investment were estimated for 1985 (see Figure 1).[22]

States also have assumed a greater role in preservation activities. Partially in response to the National Historic Preservation Act of 1966, all states created the post of state historic preservation officer; numerous states created state historic preservation registers that mirror the form, substance, and protection of the National Register of Historic Places; and most states enacted enabling legislation authorizing local government intervention in preservation efforts.

Table 1
Growth of Historic Preservation Activity: Selected Indicators

FISCAL YEAR	INDICATORS: Properties and Districts on National Register of Historic Places (entries)	Advisory Council Section 106 Review (cases)	Local Historic District Commissions	Interior Department Grants-in-Aid (millions of dollars)	FEDERAL TAX INCENTIVES FOR REHABILITATION: Rehabilitation Investment (millions of dollars)	All Projects Received
1955			20			

1966			100			
1967		0				
1968	1,204	5		$ 0.3		
1969	1,563	22		0.1		
1970	2,395	57		1.0		
1971	3,421	81		5.7		
1972	4,954	152		5.6		
1973	7,116	311		7.1		
1974	9,267	689		11.1		
1975	11,254	1,104		20.3		
1976	13,538	2,263	492	18.5		
1977	15,101	2,369		16.5		
1978	18,221	1,759	578	43.5	140*	549*
1979	21,004	2,264		58.5	300	807
1980	24,031	1,623		53.2	346	931
1981	24,549	2,700	832	26.0	738	1,654
1982	27,689	1,827	1,000	25.4	1,128	2,215
1983	32,214	2,261		26.0**	2,165	3,639
1984	36,028	2,241		26.5	2,123	4,461
1985 (est.)	37,022	2,199		26.5	2,400	4,700

* Combined fiscal years, 1977-78.
** Does not include supplemental $25 million from Jobs Bill.
Note: For local district commissions and National Register (1975 to April 1985), entries are shown by calendar, rather than fiscal, year.
Source: Diane Maddex, *The Brown Book—A Directory of Preservation Information* (Washington, D.C.: Preservation Press, 1983), pp. 33-35; interviews, National Park Service and Advisory Council, May 1985.

Figure 1
Rehabilitation Activity
Preservation Tax Incentives

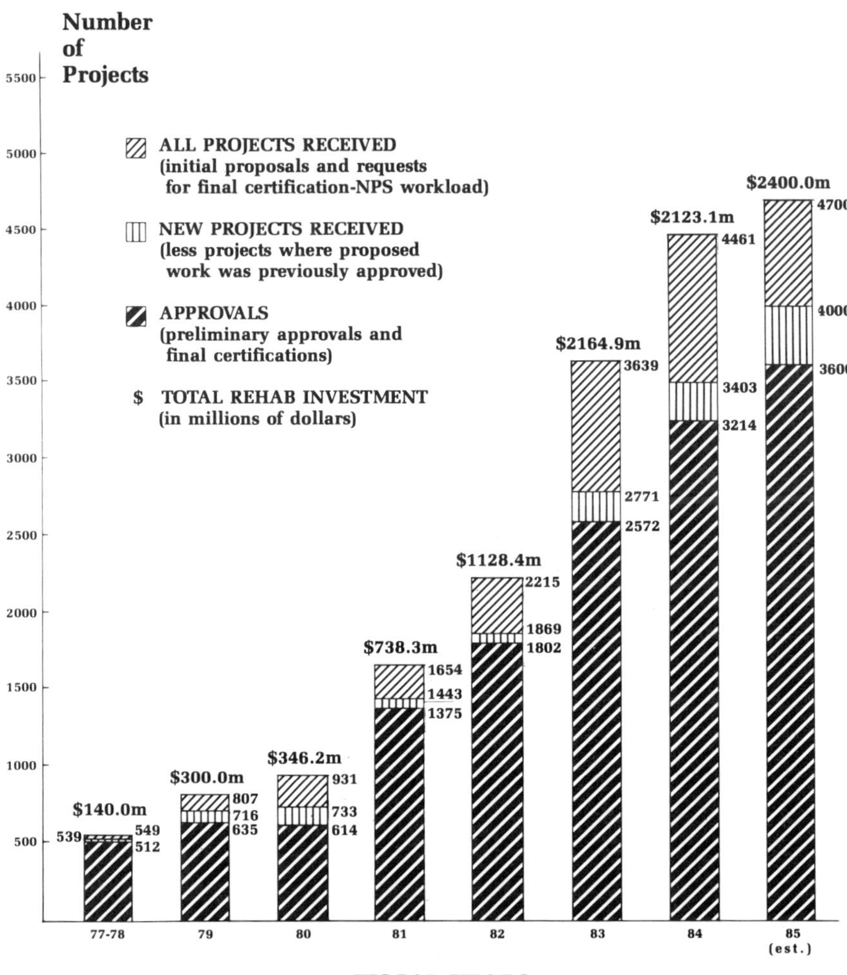

Source: Christopher A. Sowick, Preservation Assistance Division, National Park Service, U.S. Department of the Interior, January 25, 1985.

But the coming-of-age of preservation is most evident in the expansion of activity at the local government level. In 1966, approximately one hundred communities established historic district commissions with protective powers. A decade later, at the nation's bicentennial, there were five hundred such commissions. By 1982, approximately one thousand district commissions had been identified.[23] In addition to being numerous, the local commissions' powers were far-reaching. Many, for instance, were enabled by state legislation to designate architecturally or historically significant properties, thus delaying or prohibiting demolition and/or alterations.

In addition to a strong public presence, private participation is as important to preservation efforts today as in the past. It is estimated that there are approximately 4,300 preservation organizations in the United States, with a total of about two million members.[24] The largest of these groups, the National Trust for Historic Preservation, has over 125,000 members. To its supporters, there is not nearly enough advocacy for preservation—demolition and new construction still reign supreme. To its enemies, preservation has become embodied in a massive special interest group, whose breadth of focus is increasingly costly.

The concept of preservation has broadened—no longer is it limited to the best survivors or the most historic. For instance, a block of late-nineteenth-century row houses, or a factory characterizing smokestack America, might now be preserved, not because it is the fruit of any particular architectural genius or historic event, but because it is a physical legacy of the march through time.

Preservation changed in other ways. While individual buildings were still singled out for protection, groupings of structures and the overall ambience they conveyed attracted considerably greater interest—the idea developed that to preserve the past, the overall vista and composite, not only the isolated segments, had to be protected.

Still another radical change took place—a shift from preserving the past as a museum to allowing for "lived-in" historic structures. As John S. Pyke, Jr., observed in 1972, "only a few landmarks . . . can support themselves as historical museums. Most landmarks must be adapted to other uses than a public exhibition place if they are to be preserved."[25] In part, economic considerations forced this trend, as there are simply insufficient funds to maintain today's inventory of historic resources as public showplaces. But this change in orientation reflects more than the lack of dollars; it is linked to the changing concept of preservation as well. Preservation in the form of a museum becomes antithetical to maintaining a lifelike vista of the past.

Reexamination

Preservation efforts have come a long way from the early days of a limited, private activity. Today it is widely applied and involves private and increasingly public participation. The focus of preservation also has expanded from a narrow definition of "historic" to a much more encompassing view of objects deserving protection. For example, the National Register's definition of "historic" resources—incorporated by many state and local governments—is quite broad:

> Those districts, sites, buildings, structures, and objects that possess integrity of location, design, setting, materials, workmanship, feeling, and association, and (a) are associated with events that have made a significant contribution to the broad pattern of our history; or (b) that are associated with the lives of persons significant in our past; or (c) that embody distinctive characteristics of a type, period, or method of construction, or that represent the work of a master builder, or that possess high artistic value, or that represent a significant and distinguishable entity whose components may lack individual distinction; or (d) that have yielded, or may be likely to yield, information important in pre-history or history.

Given the broad interpretation of "historic"—as specifically intended by Congress in the 1966 National Historic Preservation Act—it is not surprising that National Register listings include a potpourri of items from Green Springs, Virginia, an 8,000-acre area of eighteenth- and early-nineteenth-century farms to a simple farmhouse in the Midwest; from an early skyscraper like the Wainwright Building in St. Louis to entire small towns, such as Silver Plume, Colorado. Entries range from archaeological sites, such as Cahokia Mounds in Illinois, to battlefields, such as Gettysburg and Antietam; from bridges, such as the Eads Bridge over the Mississippi, to Launch Complex 39 at Cape Canaveral; from ships, such as the schooner Wawona in Seattle, to petroglyph boulders, such as Pohaku Ka Luahine in Hawaii, to steam locomotive #152 of the Louisville and Nashville Railroad.[26]

Similarly, while at one time "preservation" meant a museum-style restoration, today, according to the secretary of the interior's standards, it is defined much more broadly, as:

> . . . generally saving from destruction or deterioration old and historic buildings, sites, structures and objects and providing for their continued use by means of restoration, rehabilitation, or adaptive use; specifically, the act or process of applying measures to sustain the existing form, integrity, and material of a building or structure, and the existing form and vegetative cover of a site. It may include stabilization work, where necessary, as well as on-going maintenance of the historic building materials.[27]

Preservation thus means many things. At its minimum, preservation avoids *demolition*. But often, it is much more. Preservation entails *maintenance*—for example, replacement of mechanical and other building systems or attention to cosmetics on a periodic basis. When maintenance is deferred for too long, or when amenities are below accepted standards or do not meet the occupants' needs, then *rehabilitation* is effected. In such instances the structure is *adaptively reused*. Examples of reuse abound—surplus schools converted to condominiums, factories made into retail boutiques, manufacturing lofts changed to offices, and so on. In other instances, the historic resource is either *restored* or *reconstructed* to its original form. Preservation thus encompasses multifaceted activities, ranging from forestalling demolition or defacement to bringing back what has been lost through restoration and reconstruction.

There is nothing wrong with the growing breadth of preservation's scope and application. Preservation should encompass more than museum restorations. Yet the growing breadth of the definition of what is important to preserve can reduce the concept to meaninglessness and lead to abuses. Preservation is not well served if it is trivialized by those claiming that much of what exists has historic virtue or if it is abused by those with a hidden agenda, such as to stop new development or to extract exactions from developers. At issue is the propriety with which local preservation commissions, the Department of the Interior, and other authorities operate with respect to their historic survey and designation work. They must resist pressure for overincorporation and must define "historic" in a consistent manner.

The growing breadth of preservation's scope and regulations raises yet another issue—the relationship of preservation to city planning. Historically, preservation and planning had distinctly different orientations: preservationists were concerned with unique individual structures, emphasized rehabilitation, and for the most part, operated in the private sector; planners, by contrast, focused on overall city conditions, encouraged new construction, and implemented zoning, building code, and other public regulations. Given these different orientations, preservationists and city planners often have been antagonistic toward one another. Over time there has been change, however. With its growing scope and applications, preservation is no longer confined to unique individual cases, nor is it excluded from the land-use regulatory sphere. City planning's orientation also has changed so as to recognize the importance of preserving individual structures and neighborhoods. How the common concerns of preservationists and city planners are handled functionally and administratively, and how preservation activities are integrated with other societal priorities, is critical to the well-being of the public at large.

Finally, the question must be asked as to whether the broadening of the preservation mandate has been for the general public good. Who really benefits—and at what (and whose) costs—from the widespread preservation activity now under way? And how effective, and equitable, are the regulations that control this growing activity?

— 2 —

Government Regulations and Supports

There is growing government involvement in historic preservation. Such action is defended as serving the public's welfare by protecting historic resources. Yet complaints are heard that the limited-range and often flawed tools available to government are insufficient to achieve the broad objectives of the preservation movement. In a different vein, others have raised serious questions, criticizing the basis and equity of the increased government participation.

The Local Government Role

Historic resources are subject to many threats: demolition by public agencies for such alternative public purposes as highways, hospitals, housing, military bases, and other construction; pressure by the real estate market to tear down and redevelop to a higher intensity of use; and the heavy financial burden on owners of historic properties to provide adequate maintenance and rehabilitation, without which deterioration and, ultimately, loss may result (i.e., "demolition by neglect," which is quite common).[1]

Current preservation measures often fall short of protecting against the many public and private threats to historic resources. It is the local government that provides the greatest protection to preservation activities, and it does so through designation. Many localities have enacted procedures whereby architecturally and/or historically significant properties can be designated as landmarks. Designation may protect the landmark by delaying or prohibiting alterations to the entire exterior, facade (the portion viewable from the street), or interior (in the case of an interior landmark), and/or demolition of the structure itself.

Changes are allowed only if they conform to the prevailing architectural style or historical motif.

No comparable controls are found at other levels of government: while federal and state regulations police government actions that might threaten historic resources, for the most part they are not directed at the owners of these resources. The significance of the local thrust has been ably summarized by John Fowler, general counsel to the Advisory Council on Historic Preservation:

> Most of the action in preservation occurs in the private sector, controlled by local regulation, and often supported by local programs. The real cutting edge of historic preservation is at the local level. [Affirmation] of these powers to regulate private property for preservation purposes came in [the] Supreme Court's decision in the celebrated Grand Central case and is expected to spawn even greater numbers of local preservation ordinances. . . . Exercising their police power . . . communities have adopted ordinances to control what the owners of historic buildings can do with their properties.[2]

Thus, for much of America, historic preservation is equated with local designation and its restrictions and supports.

Designation is a relative newcomer to the American regulatory scene. While some cities had such controls in place for decades (see Table 2), most were enacted in the early- to mid-1970s.

Designation controls are typically administered by a landmarks commission, usually with fewer than ten members, with expertise in such areas as architecture, history, art history, law, planning, and real estate. Day-to-day preservation-designation work rests on the shoulders of the commission's staff. In a recent national survey of local historic preservation commissions,* which

---

* The National Local Historic Preservation-Designation Survey consisted of telephone interviews with 160 historic preservation commissions located in small and large communities throughout the United States. This sample was selected from a national directory of over eight hundred municipalities with preservation commissions that was compiled by the National Trust for Historic Preservation. The survey thus contacted approximately 20 percent of the universe of the local historic preservation commissions in the United States as indicated in the National Trust's directory. There are an estimated one thousand local commissions today. See Stephen N. Dennis, *Directory of American Preservation Commissions* (Washington, D.C.: Preservation Press, 1981). The survey is reproduced in full in the Appendix.

Table 2
Historic Preservation Profile in Selected Major American Cities

CITY	DESIGNATION CONTROLS ADOPTED	DESIGNATION VOLUME (STRUCTURES) Today (1983)	Estimated Ten Years From Now	HISTORIC COMMISSION POWER Advise*	Delay**	Control***
Baltimore	1964	3,000	4,500			Yes
Boston	1955	2,000	2,500			Yes
Chicago	1968	6,000	12,000		Yes	
Cincinnati	1980	800	1,400			Yes
Cleveland	1971	200	600		Yes	
Dallas	1974	1,500	2,500	Yes		
Denver	1967	500	700			Yes
Detroit	1969	2,000	2,300			Yes
Indianapolis	1968	850	2,500			Yes
Kansas City	1977	750	750			Yes
Miami	1981	34	500			Yes
Milwaukee	1981	325	3,000		Yes	
New Orleans	1936	3,000	3,000			Yes
New York	1965	16,000	21,000			Yes
Oklahoma City	1974	100	200			Yes
Omaha	1977	160	300			Yes
Philadelphia	1955	8,000	10,000			Yes
San Francisco	1967	300	800			Yes
St. Paul	1976	750	1,000		Yes	
Washington, D.C.	1935	4,000	5,000			Yes

* Advisory role.
** Delay demolition/property alteration.
*** Prohibit or in other ways control demolition/property alteration.
Source: National Survey; see Appendix I.

I helped conduct and which will serve to document observations on these critical government bodies, it was discovered that, on average (median), the "staff" consisted of one to two full-time paid employees (in many instances "lent" or in other ways made available by the local planning department). This skeleton staff must handle a substantial workload. Data from the recent national survey indicate that roughly 200 of the average respondent city's structures are under historic designation, and the tally is expected to increase at a significant pace—perhaps by as much as 50 percent over the next ten years.

In order to qualify for designation as a historic building or district, a minimum age qualification, often fifty years (which mirrors the half-century requirement prescribed for entry on the National Register of Historic Places), must be met. In addition, the item must be significant from an architectural, historical, or cultural point of view.

Objects are identified through a formal historical resource inventory or survey, performed by a variety of parties such as outside consultants, the city itself, or a private historical society. Frequently the inventory or survey is not citywide but, rather, is limited to a number of promising areas. Another shortcoming is that, despite changing notions about the historic significance and classes of properties needing protection, often (in 40 percent of the cases in the recent national survey) there are no plans to update the original base inventory.

In many cases (40 percent of those surveyed), the landmarks preservation commission can designate without additional specific legislative approval. Otherwise, legislative approval as well as the recommendation of the landmarks preservation commission is required before an official imprimatur of designation is given. Owner consent and/or initiation is also required in many cases (in about half of those surveyed) before designation can be applied—perhaps in part because of the property restrictions that follow designation. Controversy arose in New York City over owner initiation and consent in the designation of property owned by St. Bartholomew's Church. Partially in response, religious leaders in New York State pressed for de-designation of properties owned by religious organizations and limiting future designation of this class of buildings to a voluntary basis. According to the recent national survey, only a handful of the 160 cities contacted—Brookhaven, New York; Central City, Colorado; Coral Gables, Florida; Independence, Missouri; and Syracuse, New York—reported that buildings owned by religious organizations required their consent for designation or in other ways were treated differently.

In the overwhelming number of cases (60 percent of those surveyed), designation can be applied both on an areawide and on an individual-building basis (i.e., dual designation), though a number of landmarks commissions (30 percent of those surveyed) can apply designation only on an areawide basis. Only a handful are limited to designation of individual buildings.

There is considerable variation in the preservation commission's exact powers—that is, what action it can take with reference to planned demolition, moving a designated structure, and alterations, as well as new construction on vacant lots in a designated neighborhood. At the least, the commission may intervene in an advisory capacity (see Table 2)—recommending actions to another body such as a city planning agency, a building department, or the local legislature. Some commissions are also empowered to delay actions threatening a designated property—for instance, by providing for a mandatory thirty-, sixty-, or ninety-day cooling-off period. But the most common, and the most stringent, preservation commission intervention is to prohibit demolition, moving, and inappropriate alterations and/or new construction. More than half of the survey respondents indicated this was the scope of their landmarks commissions' powers.

With the exception of minor maintenance, almost all work done on a designated building requires approval from the preservation commission in the form of a "Certificate of Appropriateness" or comparable permit. Action on these applications is reportedly swift. It usually takes less than one month for a petitioner to receive a Certificate of Appropriateness, although considerably longer periods of from four to six months and beyond have been reported. Eighty percent of those surveyed reported that almost all applications were approved; in the remaining cases the percentage approved was considerably less. The reasons for delay or denial range from petitions not being prepared correctly to red tape to substantive issues such as the planned alterations not being in conformity with the governing standards.

Some preservation commissions (approximately one-quarter of those surveyed) impose affirmative maintenance obligations stipulating that owners of designated buildings must keep their properties in "good" or "sound" condition—a requirement over and above that imposed by the city's general housing code that applies to all property owners. But only about two-thirds of the communities with this maintenance obligation enforce it. A number of jurisdictions (about 40 percent of those surveyed) allow for hardship relief should the owner of a designated building find it financially difficult to retain and maintain the structure in its current form. But even in the minority of jurisdictions with hardship provisions, this measure is often not specified (e.g., defining "financial hardship") and rarely applied in practice.

Enforcement of the preservation commissions' powers is generally informal—spurred by public complaints and monitored by windshield surveys taken by the commissions' staffs. Regular on-site inspection is practically nonexistent; historic preservation commissions simply do not have the personnel to formally monitor the changes taking place in the buildings under their care. There is some notification by city departments when alterations are pending, but it is minimal.

Penalties for violating designation controls are far-sweeping and nominally quite stiff. Most preservation commissions can impose fines, issue injunctions to stop unauthorized work, issue orders requiring the replacement of unauthorized changes that were not caught in time (e.g., a cornice or other decorative item removed), and, in some cases, have violators imprisoned. But these measures usually are not applied. Only 30 percent of those surveyed indicated that they imposed penalties—even in instances where they were aware of violations. This reluctance is fostered by the belief that preservation should be done on a voluntary basis by property owners who recognize the value of protecting historic resources. On a practical level, it is inadequate staffing that does not allow for pursuit of violators through the courts in order to impose fines, injunctions, etc.[3]

Because of the severe undermanning of local preservation offices and the existing tendency toward informal enforcement techniques, some slip in enforcement is likely—although its magnitude is not known. There is widespread agreement, however, that enforcement of designation-related controls certainly is not what it could be.[4]

It is clear from the above that designation, while a powerful mechanism, does not completely safeguard a historic property. It does not, for example, protect against "demolition by neglect," nor does it alleviate pressures to demolish and redevelop to a higher intensity of use. A number of other local government preservation measures could provide such relief. Transfer of Development Rights (TDR) is one such measure. A TDR program permits the sale of a property's unused development potential. For instance, under a TDR strategy, the owner of a designated historic building containing 5,000 square feet, which is located in a zone permitting a 20,000-square-foot improvement, could market 15,000 square feet of development rights. By allowing the sale of the unused development potential, TDR alleviates some of the financial pressures on the property owner.

Property tax relief is another constructive measure that local government could undertake to encourage rehabilitation by removing the threat of an increased assessment after an improvement is made. Property tax relief is now commonly used to inspire activities in the public interest—such as educational and/or cultural services provided by private, not-for-profit groups or central business district renewal. While some communities nominally extend preferred property tax treatment of historic buildings, these programs are often found wanting because of administrative inadequacies. A 1980 survey by the author found application of the historic property tax measures to be practically nil:

> The survey of practice reveals that in most cases the landmark property-tax provisions . . . have only infrequently been applied. . . . Connecticut's reduction measure has never been used; California's assessment-at-current use has also experienced minimal usage as evident from the . . . responses to a questionnaire administered by the California State Board of Equalization to the state's 58 county assessors. While almost all (55 out of 58) assessors reported the presence of eligible landmarks qualifying for the program in their counties, a negligible number (2 of 58) indicated that the landmark assessment provision was actually utilized.[5]

Property tax relief is a tool that could be much more effectively used to support historic preservation.

Public and behind-the-scenes local financial aid in the form of loans and grants—currently extended to many other theaters of activity deemed deserving of encouragement—would also foster the preservation of historic resources. Opening the door for private financing by meeting with bankers and other financial officers would also help. There is some financial aid now available on occasion: many jurisdictions draw upon their Community Development Block Grants to capitalize revolving rehabilitation loan funds. But financial support could be augmented.

Finally, technical assistance can help assure protection of historic properties by offering solutions to such difficult technical questions as: How can a cornice or other building ornamentation best be repaired? What is the architectural motif characteristic of a particular historic neighborhood? How can federal tax incentives be applied for? How can grants be secured?

But, according to the recent national survey, relatively few local communities offer the "beyond-designation" preservation measures described above (see Table 3 and the Appendix). While about 80 percent make available technical assistance, only about two-thirds offer subsidized loans and grants (when funds are available); only about one-third provide either assistance to secure private loans or extend property tax relief; and only about one-tenth allow for the sale of development rights. With the exception of technical help, owners of designated buildings are largely on their own.

Thus, while designation is an important preservation tool, it is not a quick regulatory fix—it is neither the most effective preservation mechanism nor a harmless application of the public's regulatory power. Standing alone—without being bolstered by such supports as transfer of development rights, financial aid, property tax relief, and technical assistance—designation cannot be as effective for achieving preservation aims and, worse, can be uncoordinated or even conflict with a community's overall land-use and planning vision (that officially incorporated in its master plan, zoning ordinance, and the like).[6]

If preservation influences land use, then logic dictates that preservation goals be included in the community's master (or comprehensive) plan, which provides long-range guidance for the growth and development of a community in terms of population, economy, housing, transportation, community facilities, and land use.

Communities implement their land-use vision through zoning, which controls the uses permitted and the intensity of development allowed; through subdivision standards, which affect the division of land for sale, development, or lease; and through the building code, which establishes the building materials used and/or techniques and standards applied for new construction and/or rehabilitation. This land-use regulatory structure—zoning, subdivision, and building codes—has a bear-

Table 3
Historic Preservation Profile in Selected Major American Cities

	SCOPE: IS THE FOLLOWING ASSISTANCE OFFERED?					LINKAGE: HISTORIC PRESERVATION ACTIVITY LINKED TO OR COORDINATED WITH THE COMMUNITY'S:			
CITY	TDR	Property Tax Relief	Subsidized Loans	Other Financial Aid	Technical Aid	Comprehensive Plan	Zoning Ordinance	Subdivision Ordinance	Building Code
Baltimore	No	No	Yes	No	Yes	Yes	No	No	Yes
Boston	No	No	Yes	Yes	Yes	Yes	Yes	No	Yes
Chicago	No	Yes	Yes	Yes	Yes	No	No	No	No
Cincinnati	No	No	Yes	No	Yes	Yes	No	No	Yes
Cleveland	No	No	Yes	Yes	Yes	Yes	Yes	Yes	Yes
Dallas	Yes	Yes	Yes	No	Yes	Yes	Yes	No	Yes
Denver	Yes	No	No	No	Yes	Yes	Yes	No	Yes
Detroit	No	No	Yes	No	Yes	Yes	Yes	Yes	No
Indianapolis	No	Yes	No	No	Yes	Yes	Yes	No	No
Kansas City	No	Yes	Yes	No	Yes	No	No	No	No
Miami	Yes	No	Yes	No	No	No	No	No	No
Milwaukee	No	No	No	No	Yes	No	No	No	Yes
New Orleans	No	Yes	No	No	Yes	Yes	Yes	No	Yes
New York	Yes	Yes	Yes	No	Yes	Yes	Yes	No	No
Oklahoma City	No	No	No	No	Yes	No	No	No	No
Omaha	No	No	Yes	Yes	Yes	Yes	No	No	No
Philadelphia	No	No	No	No	Yes	No	No	No	Yes
San Francisco	Yes	No	Yes	No	Yes	Yes	Yes	No	No
St. Paul	No	No	No	No	Yes	Yes	No	No	No
Washington, D.C.	No	Yes	No	No	Yes	Yes	Yes	No	Yes

Source: National Survey; see Appendix I.

ing on historic preservation. If the zoning code allows a high intensity of use, it imposes pressure for the demolition and redevelopment in historic buildings, which typically reflect the lesser intensity of use of the past. Density bonuses for plazas and other amenities can have the same effect. If the subdivision ordinance mirrors the ideal of tract suburbia, then new developments at the edge of historic districts clash with the ambience preserved within the historic neighborhood. Building code requirements can add significantly to the costs of rehabilitating historic properties if strict new building standards (e.g., governing stairway width, exterior finish, etc.—changes that are expensive to retrofit in historic properties) are applied.

While historic preservation is best fostered by coordinating designation with the community's land-use statement—the master plan—the recent national survey points to the frequent absence of such coordination. Only about half of the respondents claimed some association, and this, typically, was more form than substance (e.g., mention of the term "historic preservation" in the comprehensive plan among other community goals). Even fewer respondents (about 40 percent) pointed to any links between designation and zoning, subdivision, and building codes, and where they existed the association was often faint (e.g., a clause in a building code that allows for some exemption for historic properties provided the basis for such exemption could be substantiated). Here, again, is an area where the local government role should be reexamined.

Still another area where there is inadequate coordination and linkage is that of identifying historic resources. The federal, state, and local governments are all involved in historic designation and protection activities. But activities of the different levels of government are often not well coordinated. Efforts to foster closer integration are being made. For example, the 1980 amendments to the federal National Historic Preservation Act provided for the "certification" of local governments. Such "certification" allows for a closer partnership among the federal, state, and local governments.

The Federal Government

The federal government has assumed a leadership and educational role in preservation activities by virtue of the value it places on historic resources. One of the ways in which it has encouraged the pursuit of preservation activities is through the creation of federal historic surveys and designation processes—the most significant being the National Register of Historic Places. Much of the Register's documentary and review procedures actually are performed by state governments, but such state involvement is promoted by federal financial aid—in the form of matching grants—from the National Historic Preservation Fund. This fund supports state surveys for historic properties, formulation of historic preservation plans, preparation of nominations to the National Register, acquisition and maintenance of properties listed on the Register, and the staffing of the State Historic Preservation Office and the position of state historic preservation officer (SHPO).[7]

Through the National Historic Preservation Fund, the federal government also supports the National Trust for Historic Preservation—a private, not-for-profit organization chartered by Congress in 1949—whose mission is to encourage private participation in preservation by serving as an information clearinghouse, by coordinating preservation group activities, by maintaining historic properties, and by conducting legal and other research.[8]

Federal agencies themselves have become sensitized to preservation by virtue of Executive Order 11593, which requires them to locate, inventory, and nominate buildings and other objects within their control to the National Register; the Public Buildings Cooperative Use Act, which requires them to use, "to the maximum extent feasible, historic properties available to them"; as well as other legislation.

Once a historical resource has been identified, the federal government offers it some protection by requiring that any federal action that could adversely affect the resource be subject to review processes. The most significant of these is the Section 106 review, mandated by the National Historic Preservation Act (NHPA) of 1966.

Section 106 review is triggered by a federal "undertaking"—that is, "any federal, federally-assisted, or federally-licensed action, activity, or program or the approval, sanction, assistance, or support of any non-federal action, activity, or program."[9] Following the determination that an activity constitutes a federal "undertaking," Section 106 requires that the state historic preservation officer and the federal agency planning the undertaking identify existing or potential historic resources that may be affected by it.

The next step is to consider whether the undertaking will have no effect on the historic resource, no adverse effect, or an adverse effect. In a finding of "no effect" or "no adverse effect," the federal agency proceeds with the project, keeping a record of the finding. In the case of an "adverse" or "hostile" effect, a consultation process begins, which brings together the state historic preservation officer and the federal agency contemplating the action, with the Advisory Council on Historic Preservation acting as mediator. The result of this consultation is typically a Memorandum of Agreement (MOA)—a product of compromise. Where an MOA cannot be agreed upon, the matter goes before the full council for review and recommendation.[10]

But while the Section 106 process is obligatory, it can in no way prohibit federal activity that negatively affects the historic environment. Having satisfied the Section 106 procedure, nothing forces a federal agency to agree to requests from the Advisory Council that historic resources be spared.

Under the Reagan administration, as part of a comprehensive review of federal controls, the Office of Management and Budget (OMB) examined the Section 106 review process and formally indicated its displeasure at alleged project implementation delays. In response, the Advisory Council drafted regulations to expedite the procedure, but OMB rejected these proposals, charging that the process was too time-consuming and unnecessarily altered federal undertakings. OMB further charged that the process is illegal. According to Christopher DeMuth, OMB's administrator for information and regulatory affairs, NHPA called for the Advisory Council to "comment" on the effect of federal activity on historic resources, and mandated that the comment be "taken into account" by the federal agencies;[11] it did not indicate the detailed review procedure and MOA. Thus, according to OMB, not only is the Section 106 process working poorly, but it has no basis in law. The Advisory Council, however, which views itself as neutral, contends that a "negotiated solution" and its "conflict resolution role" are de facto called for, if not explicitly required, by NHPA, and claims that the process works expeditiously and economically. Of the 78,800 federal undertakings subject to Section 106 review in fiscal year 1984, all but 2,300 were resolved at the state level; only about 200 cases required substantial consultation by the Advisory Council staff before an MOA was reached.

This dispute between OMB and the Advisory Council, while unresolved, illustrates the growing concern with, and influence of, government involvement in historic preservation. Until the past decade, there were few significant preservation regulations, and the handful available were gingerly applied by preservationists unsure of the regulations' legal status or political acceptability. This state of affairs has changed dramatically; today there are numerous public regulations, most of which have a strong legal sign-off by the judiciary.

A second federal review process with respect to preservation was initiated by the National Environmental Policy Act (NEPA) of 1969. NEPA gives the federal government the responsibility "to preserve and enhance the environment including the *historic*, cultural, and natural aspects of our national heritage." NEPA is implemented via the environmental impact statement (EIS), which bears similarities to the Section 106 process. It, too, is triggered by specified federal activity—namely, "major federal actions significantly affecting the quality of the human environment." The EIS is a detailed statement, prepared by the federal agency undertaking the action, consisting of a description of the intended action and possible alternatives; a description of the affected environment; an analysis of the environmental consequences, both that of the intended action and of the alternatives; and a discussion of measures to limit harmful effects on the environment. In the case of a federal action that will negatively affect a historic resource, the EIS, if properly prepared, will define the level and type of effect, consider alternative actions more amenable to the historic environment, and/or, if the original action is to be maintained, analyze how its adverse effects can be mitigated.

But, again, preparation of an EIS is a procedural stipulation. NEPA does not halt activity harmful to the environment—historic or otherwise. NEPA requires only that the effects be considered in an EIS with alternatives and mitigating actions noted. Having filed an EIS, a federal agency is free to demolish or in other ways to "adversely affect the historic environment." Thus, while both NEPA and the Section 106 process require that some attention be paid by federal agencies to historic preservation, they do not prohibit destructive actions.

A more stringent federal stipulation is provided by Section 4(f) of the Department of Transportation Act of 1966, which forbids the use of any land, private or public, for federal highway purposes from an historic site unless there is no "prudent and feasible alternative to the use of such land," and requires that "all possible planning to minimize harm" be "accomplished."[12]

In some ways, Section 4(f) offers the highest level of federal protection of historic resources, but it affects only the Department of Transportation; other agencies must adhere only to the less-demanding Section 106 and EIS procedures. Thus, while Section 106, NEPA, and Section 4(f) are all important regulations, they are, for the most part, procedural. If federal agencies are to protect historic resources, they must incorporate this goal in their planning. Planning is the key.

To private property owners, the most significant federal preservation measure is financial support—provided in the form of tax incentives. First granted by the 1976 Tax Reform Act, tax incentives for preservation activity were expanded by the Economic Recovery Tax Act (ERTA) of 1981, which provides for Investment Tax Credits (ITCs) for the rehabilitation of income-producing buildings. (A credit differs from a depreciation write-off in that a one-dollar credit reduces the tax liability by an equivalent amount, while the value of a dollar of depreciation depends on the taxpayer's bracket. For example, a one-dollar write-off is worth fifty cents to someone in the 50 percent tax bracket; twenty-five cents to someone in the 25 percent tax bracket, etc.) As reflected by its growing utilization, the ITC has proved to be a powerful investment lure.

ERTA provides for a three-tier ITC: a 15 percent ITC is allowed for rehabilitation of commercial buildings that are at least 30 years old; a 20 percent ITC is granted for the rehabilitation of commercial buildings at least 40 years old; and a 25 percent ITC is available for improving income-producing (residential and commercial) certified historic structures.*

The ITC, in all three cases, is limited to "qualified rehabilitated buildings." To qualify, the structure has to be "substantially rehabilitated"—which entails a renovation outlay of the greater of either $5,000 or the adjusted basis of the property (purchase price and improvements, less depreciation). The structure must retain 75 percent of its external walls, and must be completely rehabilitated within a 24-month period. Further, expenditures must be for significant construction, as opposed to maintenance

---

* That is, structures that are individually listed on the National Register of Historic Places, located in a district listed on the National Register, or located in a district designated under a state or local statute certified by the secretary of the interior as containing criteria substantially in conformity with the National Register.

items. In addition, to qualify for the 25 percent ITC, further provisions must be satisfied: not only must the building be a "certified historic structure" but the planned rehabilitation must be "certified" as architecturally appropriate.

In addition to claiming the rehabilitation tax credit, the owner of a substantially rehabilitated income-producing building (either a historic or a nonhistoric building) can depreciate his holdings for tax purposes. This depreciation (technically, Accelerated Cost Recovery) is especially significant with regard to historic resources. In cases of nonhistoric rehabilitation—where the 15 or 20 percent ITC is used—the depreciable basis (i.e., total property value) is reduced by the full amount of the credit, hence less tax shelter is provided. In contrast, in applying the 25 percent ITC for rehabilitation of a historic structure, the depreciable basis is reduced by only one-half the amount of the credit, thus allowing a greater remaining depreciable basis.

Figure 2 shows the steadily increasing number of projects and growth in rehabilitation investment in historic buildings since 1976. Not surprisingly, given the enhanced incentives offered by ERTA, the volume has been most impressive in the years following ERTA's enactment in 1981. As of the first quarter of fiscal year 1985, 11,512 projects nationwide have qualified for historic preservation rehabilitation incentives, representing an estimated $7.63 billion of rehabilitation work.[13] An estimated 60,000 housing units were involved in the rehabilitation process since 1976, including the creation of almost 32,000 new housing units. About 14,000 of these units were slated for low- and moderate-income families. Roughly one-half of the rehabilitated projects were for housing purposes; 21 percent were rehabilitated for mixed-use purposes; 16 percent were rehabilitated for office space; 8 percent were intended strictly for commercial enterprises; 2 percent of all projects were hotel rehabilitations; and 2 percent were for other miscellaneous uses.[14]

Yet, while federal tax policy provides a considerable tax incentive for owners of historic buildings, some of its governing provisions limit its effectiveness—often in the very instances where it may be most appropriate or needed. For instance, non-income-producing historic properties—such as residences—are not eligible for the ITC even in instances where rehabilitation is needed, yet may not be affordable.

The "substantial rehabilitation" requirement also often has undesirable effects. In a borderline case of eligibility, an investor is encouraged to increase the rehabilitation outlay just to satisfy the "substantial rehabilitation" threshold; this extra renovation adds to carrying costs and often has little substantive benefit. The measure is especially counterproductive when the property owner is financially pressed. The "substantial rehabilitation" test also may discourage investment on the part of new property owners whose adjusted basis is likely to be high, as opposed to long-term owners whose adjusted basis has been lowered by multiyear depreciation. Disqualifying new owners from using the ITC is shortsighted because this group offers much in the way of initiative and energy. In addition, the "substantial rehabilitation" test can restrict eligibility for the ITC in strong real estate markets where purchase prices and, therefore, the adjusted basis, are high. It is in these markets that historic properties are faced with the most severe redevelopment pressures and thus would benefit from federal tax support. According to a recent report by the Advisory Council on Historic Preservation:

> Research shows that the 25 percent ITC is used significantly less in cities in which strong real-estate markets have kept values of commercial properties high. In New York City, only thirteen applications were submitted for the 25 percent credit in 1982. By comparison, 38 projects were submitted from Albany.[15]

Thus federal tax incentives have made great strides in encouraging the rehabilitation of historic buildings. They have reversed a long-standing bias in the federal tax code favoring new construction. Yet, as currently construed, the federal historic preservation tax incentives are sometimes found wanting in the very cases where they are most needed.

In addition to tax credits, the federal government offers direct financial support for historic preservation activities (e.g., the National Historic Preservation Fund, National Park Service, and the like) and indirect or partial financial support (e.g., through Community Development Block Grants of the Department of Housing and Urban Development, and funding for the National Foundation on the Arts and Humanities, etc.). The specific dollar support through indirect and partial support programs is broader and therefore very difficult to estimate; we can, however, define the dollar commitment provided by direct support and tax credits (foregone tax revenue). The federal financial commitment to preservation is indicated in Table 4. Data indicate the following trends:

Federal Support for Historic Preservation
Targeted Programs
(in millions of dollars)

Fiscal Year	Tax Assistance (foregone revenue)	Direct Support	Total Support
1981	120	62	182
1982	185	71	256
1983	270	75	345
1984	310	78	388
1985	325	78	403
1986*	325	50	375

*(proposed/estimated)

The overall trend is clearly upward. But if the powerhouse federal tax aid were deleted, the federal financial commitment would not be that extensive in terms of total dollars. To give some sense of scale, in fiscal year 1985, the National Historic Preservation Fund—one of the most important direct federal financial aids to preservation—amounted to roughly $25 million. In the same year, foregone tax revenue as a result of the ITC amounted to over $300 million—twelve times as much (see Table 4).

Further, direct federal financial aid to preservation is being threatened by severe cuts—a change reflecting the lowered domestic spending of the Reagan administration. Still, even in its reduced form, preservation today draws from the federal budget much more significantly than it did in the past.

The question that must be addressed is whether federal financial aid to preservation should consist overwhelmingly of a tax mechanism. Would a more flexible financial aid program—one making available loans or even grants in cases of need (e.g., non-income-producing historic buildings requiring rehabilitation or historic structures with maintenance problems)—be more appropriate? A shift away from the current emphasis on tax incentives would offer the advantage of making the true public cost of preservation better known and controllable, as program outlays could be more readily projected and adjusted than can revenue lost by a tax program. But a shift from an ITC to direct assistance would substantially increase administrative costs. And the ITC has proved a most potent rehabilitation incentive.

Table 4
Federal Financial Support for Historic Preservation: Major Targeted Programs—Estimated (in millions of dollars)

CATEGORY OF SUPPORT	FISCAL YEAR 1981	1982	1983	1984	1985	1986 (proposed)
I—DIRECT SUPPORT—APPROPRIATIONS						
Advisory Council for Historic Preservation	1.6	1.6	1.5	1.6	1.5	1.2
National Park Service						
Historic Preservation Fund[1]	26.0	25.4	26.0	26.5	25.5	0.0
Surveys and Technical Assistance[2]	4.6	4.6	4.5	5.6	6.7	6.7
Park Cultural Resources[3]	30.2	39.1	43.2	44.1	44.1	42.5
TOTAL DIRECT SUPPORT—APPROPRIATIONS	62.4	70.7	75.2	77.8	77.8	50.4
II-DIRECT SUPPORT—TAX INCENTIVES						
Internal Revenue Service[4]	120.0	185.0	270.0	310.0	325.0	325.0
TOTAL DIRECT SUPPORT—TAX	120.0	185.0	270.0	310.0	325.0	325.0
TOTAL COMBINED DIRECT SUPPORT (Appropriations and Tax Incentives)	182.4	255.7	345.2	387.8	402.8	375.4

* The exhibit does *not* include preservation assistance for archaeology and other areas provided by such agencies as HUD, Army Corps of Engineers and the Bureau of Land Management.

Notes:
[1]For National Trust for Historic Preservation and state programs; does not include supplemental $25 million added by Jobs Bill.
[2]For National Register of Historic Places, Historic American Building Survey, Historic American Engineering Record, Technical Preservation Series.
[3]For regional operations, regular and cyclical maintenance, etc.; does not include construction funding.
[4]In terms of foregone tax revenue, FY 1986 is estimated.

Source: Derived from the National Park Service, May 1985; National Trust for Historic Preservation, "The Preservation Budget of the United States, Fiscal Year 1985." Prepared by Kate M. Perry, February 17, 1983; and Executive Office of the President, Office of Management and Budget, *Special Analyses—Budget of the United States Government—Fiscal Year 1985* (Washington, D.C.: Government Printing Office, 1984), pp. G-31 and 32.

Another question that must be addressed is whether, with limited resources available for preservation purposes, it would not be best to target tax incentive programs toward cases of greatest need and/or on the most significant of the historic inventory. Currently, this is not done.

Under the present regulations, once the threshold tests of "certified structure," "certified rehabilitation," "substantial rehabilitation," and so on, are met, the project automatically qualifies for ITC assistance. No differentiation is made between projects that "need" federal tax support and those that likely would proceed in its absence. Thus rehabilitation of luxury housing garners as much federal tax support as units provided for families of more modest means. Historic preservation projects in the most affluent areas of a city are treated the same as renovation in "inner" city areas. (Certain ITC requirements, such as the "substantial rehabilitation" test, may indirectly work to discourage utilization of the ITC for rehabilitation of luxury projects in affluent neighborhoods.) Yet it must be acknowledged that greater targeting of ITC assistance would add to administrative delays and costs.

The State Role

State government plays a significant role in historic preservation by authorizing local jurisdictions (that do not possess home-rule powers) to engage in various preservation activities—the most important being local designation of individual landmarks and/or historic districts.[16] Many states also allow local preservation commissions and governing bodies to acquire historic sites on a full-fee and a less-than-fee arrangement (such as a preservation easement).[17] More than thirty states authorize localities to grant preferred property tax treatment for historic preservation purposes. Examples range from providing total tax exemption to local not-for-profit preservation societies to not reassessing historic properties following their rehabilitation.

States also serve as the operating arm of the federal preservation thrust. The focal agency of this federal/state nexus is the state historic preservation officer. Among the responsibilities of the SHPO are to compile and maintain a statewide survey and inventory of historic properties; implement a statewide historic preservation plan; administer federal assistance to the state grants-in-aid programs; aid federal, state, and local governments in carrying out their historic preservation duties; identify, nominate, and process eligible properties for listing on the National Register; work with the secretary of the interior, the Advisory Council on Historic Preservation, and federal and state agencies to ensure that historic properties are considered throughout planning and development; serve as an information, education, training, and technical source for federal and state historic preservation programs; participate in the Section 106 process; and approve eligibility for federal rehabilitation tax credits.[18]

While the thrust of state activity is to allow the local government to act or to implement federally mandated and/or financed preservation programs, some states have taken a more activist role. For instance, California, Hawaii, Illinois, Kansas, New York, and a handful of others have State Registers of Historic Places—a roster of items of state significance.[19] Frequently accompanying this is a "mini-Section 106'' process. Like its federal namesake, the state 106 review examines government action inimical to entries on the state register. Some states also have "mini-NEPAs" that, as at the federal level, mandate that an environmental impact statement be prepared to examine the effects of major state actions. Such state requirements, however, are the exception rather than the rule. Even in these instances, state intervention has been influenced by the federal format and catalyzed by federal grants-in-aid. Thus the state role in historic preservation is that of a "sleeping giant."

— 3 —

Effects

Doubts about historic district designation have proved unfounded. . . . Designation does not stop the clock. It does not freeze development.

— Jane Trichter[1]

To protect specific buildings is historic preservation; to petrify 60 busy square blocks is urban planning run amok.

— Daniel Rose[2]

The adaptation for modern use of historically and culturally important buildings gives the people who use them and live with them a sense of contact with the American heritage.

— Advisory Council on Historic Preservation[3]

Planners may argue over the causes of displacement, and we as preservationists may reject the label of gentrifiers, but to many Americans who live in inner-city neighborhoods, we are the cause of the problem.

— Michael D. Ainslie[4]

Preservationists have long argued the intangible social benefits inherent in preserving the past.[5] By conserving the historical and physical legacy, they claim, preservation provides a reassuring chain of continuity between people today and their forebears.[6] Many observers, pointing to the rapidity of change in American society—change in where we live, how we think, what we aspire to, and so on—have noted a yearning for some bedrock of permanence that can be satisfied through preservation. Robert Stipe, one of the founding fathers of the modern-day preservation movement, reported that "I have come to believe that the urge to preserve is less rooted in high-style cultural soil than in a more fundamental, even biological need all of us have to try to reduce or moderate the pace and scale of change itself."[7]

Some have espoused preservation as fostering a sense of belonging and a collective identity. It has been said that "the quality of life in a city is more dependent on the need for identity than many people realize. . . . Gertrude Stein's celebrated comment, 'There is no there, there' upon seeing Oakland, California, in 1934, identified what has already become a national problem."[8] President Franklin D. Roosevelt praised preservation for inspiring patriotism: "The preservation of historic sites for the public benefit, together with their proper interpretation, tend to enhance the respect and love of the citizen for the institutions of the country, as well as strengthen his resolution to defend unselfishly the hallowed traditions and high ideals of America."[9]

Preservation has also been praised for providing a living laboratory—a "three-dimensional record of the tastes and values affecting daily lives in the past"[10]—and for protecting the American birthright. According to Stipe, "We seek to preserve the architecture and landscapes of the past simply because of their intrinsic value as art. These structures and areas were designed by some of America's greatest artists. They are as important to our artistic heritage as our decorative arts, our painting and sculpture."[11]

Preservation is also celebrated for allowing a veil of beauty to rest over the squalor dominating the vista of many American cities.[12] Even when clean and new, the contemporary American-built environment is often viewed as inadequate, especially when contrasted to the textural and humanistic qualities successfully conveyed by architects in the past. As Paul Goldberger, architectural critic for *The New York Times*, stated:

> A great deal of the force of the preservation movement comes from contemporary architecture's failure to build well, its failure to build in a style that satisfies the needs of our cities and the needs of our senses. A lot of our belief in preservation comes from our fear of what will replace buildings that are not preserved; all too often, we fight to save not because what we want to save is so good, but because we know that what will replace it will be no better.[13]

But while few would argue with these intangible social benefits, the more tangible effects of the blossoming preservation movement have been mixed. Benefits have been achieved, but often at real costs.

Property Values

On a very practical, specific level, preservation has had a significant impact on property values.[14] On the positive side, landmark status accords prestige, through official recognition that a building or area has special qualities. In addition, local designation adds a protective overlay to a landmarked property or area: it reduces the threat of disruptive demolition from highway construction, urban renewal, and other government-aided projects; it allows alteration of landmark exteriors only only if proposed changes are compatible from architectural and other perspectives (in some cases, landmark interiors have the same protection); and it regulates new construction on vacant lots in historic districts. Thus designation increases the likelihood that the features one finds attractive in a building or an area today will be there tomorrow.

But local designation also can have an adverse effect on property values. (Federal and state preservation regulations pose few if any limitations on the owners of designated properties.) For example, landmark status may require retention and/or repair of difficult-to-maintain facades—terra cotta, tile, and gilded exteriors, as well as decorative treatments such as cornices, parapets, and ironwork—which in a nonlandmarked building might be removed and replaced by more modern finishes that are less costly to maintain. Landmark owners also may incur additional expenses as a result of having to comply with regulatory requirements: alterations and/or demolition of properties accorded historic status must be approved by the local preservation commission, and work can proceed only after a Certificate of Appropriateness has been applied for and issued. The result is added outlays for professional (i.e., architectural and legal) assistance, and possibly costly delays attendant to such administrative procedures.

It should be noted that not all owners of landmark buildings are affected by the added expense of facade maintenance and of complying with alteration and/or demolition administrative procedures. Usually, it is only in select cases, where frequent property alterations occur. Typically, moreover, the added outlays associated with landmark status will not be very significant. But, in some instances, the controls granted local preservation commissions over the alteration and/or demolition of landmark buildings can have a severe effect on property values.

A site's potential income, and therefore its value, is affected by the intensity of use to which it may be improved; all other things being equal, the higher the intensity, the greater the potential income value. Landmark status and attendant restrictions on alteration and/or demolition can curtail a site's intensity of use to its current application. This "freeze" will adversely affect property value in those cases where profitability could otherwise have been enhanced by demolition of the existing structure and replacement by one with a higher intensity of use. Such restriction on development is particularly felt in the case of uneconomic improvement—a property that is drastically underimproved as far as its intensity of use is concerned, given conventional zoning allowances and market demand—such as a small residential townhouse in a central business district. Thus designation can drastically lower property value because it disallows replacement by more profitable use.

The property-value-reducing effect of preservation controls has raised the question of whether landmark regulations violate constitutional protections against the taking of property. The lead case on this matter is *Penn Central Transportation Company v. New York City*, which concerns the landmarking and use of Grand Central Station in New York City—completed in 1913 and designated a landmark, as one of the best examples of French Beaux-Arts, in August 1967.[15]

In an attempt to capitalize on the train station's unused development potential, Penn Central, the owner of the terminal, prepared two (similar) plans for constructing high-rise office space on the roof of the station and submitted the plans to the Landmarks Preservation Commission. The stakes were high, as Grand Central occupies more than two full blocks of mid-Manhattan real estate—one of the most valuable real estate areas in the world. The commission rejected both proposals as inappropriate to the terminal's design and ambience. In response, Penn Central challenged the constitutionality of New York City's landmark law. Among other arguments, it claimed that designation constituted a taking of property.

In 1978, by a six-justice majority, the U.S. Supreme Court affirmed the designation of the terminal, noting that cities had the right to enhance their quality of life by preserving aesthetic features.[16] The test as to whether the designation of Grand Central (with attendant restrictions on demolition and other changes) was a taking of property followed that used in considering zoning effects—namely, that in the absence of land use-restrictions, controls would be upheld if they allowed for some economic use, albeit not the most profitable one possible. Under this test, the Supreme Court ruled that the designation of Grand Central did not constitute a taking:

> The New York City law does not interfere in any way with the present uses of the Terminal. Its designation as a landmark not only permits but contemplates that appellants may continue to use the property precisely as it has for the past 65 years: as a railroad terminal containing open space and concessions. So the law does not interfere with what must be regarded as Penn Central's primary expectation concerning the use of the parcel. More importantly, for the present case, in instances in which a state tribunal reasonably concluded that "the health, safety, morals, or general welfare" would be promoted by prohibiting particular contemplated uses of land, this court has upheld land use regulations that destroyed or severely affected recognized real property interests.[17]

If a landmark ceases to be "economically viable," however, the Supreme Court decision allows the owner to seek relief.

While *Penn Central* is truly a "landmark" decision with respect to historic preservation, it does not conclusively resolve the issue of designation's effect on property rights. For one thing, the judiciary's view on this matter may change. The *Penn Central* decision may reflect a U.S. Supreme Court that was more amenable to public control than it is today and, especially, than it will be tomorrow. We are already witnessing some retrenchment by the justices in recent rulings concerning public land-use regulations (e.g., *San Diego Gas & Electric*).[18]

Some state courts may be proceeding in the same direction. For instance, in Chicago, a property owner received demolition permits, but these were revoked by the Chicago Commission on Historical and Architectural Landmarks on the grounds that the buildings were being considered for designation. The owner challenged, claiming that preservation regulations had gone "too far." A circuit court in Cook County agreed, ruling the landmark ordinance unconstitutional and void.[19]

While isolated examples on the judicial landscape, the San Diego and Chicago cases cannot be ignored, because they raise lingering questions about the bounds of land-use regulations when they affect property rights.[20]

Designation's effect on the value and use of properties owned by not-for-profit and religious organizations has also come to the fore. These groups are often housed in older, architecturally distinctive structures, commonly designated as historic landmarks. Since designation can prohibit demolition and redevelopment to a higher intensity of use, leaders of these groups have charged that designation forces them to remain in buildings that are no longer suitable to their needs, that no longer sustain their organizational and religious ministries.[21] In response, preservationists claim that designation has little bearing on the suitability of a property to an organization's needs, and in instances where it does, provisions within the designation system provide necessary relief.[22]

This issue has already come to the judicial forum, though without resolution. In 1974, for instance, the United Lutheran Church challenged the designation of its Manhattan headquarters, located in the former home of J. P. Morgan, Jr., in *Lutheran Church in America v. City of New York*. The case came before the New York Court of Appeals, which ruled that the designation should be lifted, stating that the Morgan mansion was "totally inadequate for the church's administrative needs."[23] In a more recent decision, however, *Society for Ethical Culture v. Spatt*, the New York Court of Appeals found that the landmark designation of the meeting house of the Society for Ethical Culture did not seriously interfere with that group's charitable purposes.[24]

Considerable publicity has attended the case of St. Bartholomew's Church in midtown Manhattan, one of the first designated landmark buildings in New York City, which wants to demolish its landmark-status community house in order to construct a fifty-nine story office tower.[25] While the church claims that it needs the rent it would receive from the office tower to continue its ministry, preservationists have discounted this cry of poverty; if St. Bartholomew's is financially pressed, they argue, it should seek redress under New York City's landmark hardship provision.[26] It is likely that this controversy will be decided in a judicial forum. In the meantime, it has led to advocacy for state legislation that would de-landmark already-designated religious properties and make future designation of such buildings contingent upon the religious groups' agreement to such action. If enacted, this New York State legislation would join a municipal statute in Independence, Missouri, where special treatment has been established for the designation of properties owned by religious organizations.

Even if designation is fully compatible with First Amendment and other legal safeguards, the search for preservation mechanisms that have less of an adverse impact on property value should continue. For instance, a transfer of development rights program—an idea discussed but little implemented in the United States—could provide relief. Also, local assessors could (and by law should) value landmarks commensurate with their redevelopment restrictions, not at a "highest and best use" that they may not be able to attain.

Urban Revitalization

Historic designation, by regulating alterations, demolition, and new construction, may impede efforts at urban revitalization. Most studies, however, stress the positive link between preservation and revitalization of the nation's cities. In fact, many of the leading examples of residential urban turnabout in the United States—Brooklyn Heights and Park Slope in New York City, Society Hill in Philadelphia, and Beacon Hill in Boston—have occurred in areas of historic interest. The same is true of numerous nonresidential rehabilitation success stories—Boston's Faneuil Hall, San Francisco's Ghirardelli Square, and Denver's Larimer Square. Thus historic preservation activities in general, and designation in particular, are considered significant contributors to city revitalization.

In 1979, the Advisory Council on Historic Preservation examined four historic neighborhoods—Alexandria, Virginia's Old Towne Historic District; Galveston, Texas's Strand neighborhood; Savannah, Georgia's National Landmark area; and Seattle, Washington's Pioneer Square—concluding that "Preservation activities have revitalized urban historic districts while conserving valuable older properties."[27] Preservation was linked to a dramatic increase in physical renovation activity, the formation of new businesses, the stimulation of investment of private funds and lending, an increase in tourism, a decrease in crime, a significant rise in property values, and an overall improvement in the quality of life. By contrast, areas that had not caught the attention of preservationists had not exhibited comparable revitalization. For instance, property value appreciation in the historic neighborhoods consistently outdistanced that in nonhistoric areas. The more recent national survey of local historic preservation commissions also strongly supports the preservation-neighborhood revitalization link. Developers, on the other hand, often do not share this point of view—to put it mildly. The controversy over the Urban Development Action Grant (UDAG) is illustrative.

UDAG, an economic revitalization program started in 1977 and administered by the Department of Housing and Urban Development, awards grants to cities that, in turn, use these funds to attract commercial, housing, and other private investments—typically in downtown locations. Thus far, UDAG has been quite successful. It has also stirred considerable debate about how best to renew urban centers. Many UDAG proposals embrace the philosophy of the new—the convention center, hotel, shopping center, for example—as the only realistic way to attract businesses and people to downtown locations. Preservationists charge that UDAG is urban renewal in drag and is repeating its predecessor's mistake of demolishing what is uniquely urban and replacing it with poor imitations of an inappropriate suburban landscape.

For instance, conflict arose over a UDAG-financed project—Canal Place, a major hotel-office redevelopment—built in the nation's first historic district, the Vieux Carré in New Orleans. The scale of the development, its impact on traffic within the historic district, and its visual impact on the very special architectural and historical ambience of the Vieux Carré all sparked considerable controversy. Further, preservationists feared that an unbridled Canal Place would foster comparable development and sound the death knell for the district. For his part, the Canal Place developer contended that the concessions preservationists were seeking (e.g., a reduction in tower height) would have made the undertaking uneconomical.

The preservation versus UDAG redevelopment drama also came to Broadway. UDAG monies are helping to revitalize the tawdry Times Square area by financing the fifty-story Portman Hotel—a project that required the demolition of the noted Helen Hayes and Morosco theaters. Proponents of the project claim that the jobs generated, the increase in the ratable base, and area revitalization justified demolition of the theaters, but preservationists maintain that a change in plan could have saved the theaters while allowing the admittedly beneficial project to proceed.

Preservation versus UDAG new-construction conflicts became so common that in 1980, the Wylie Amendment was adopted to expedite Section 106 reviews with respect to UDAG projects.[28] Still, tensions continue over preservation's effect on urban revitalization. Proponents of new construction contend that while the past must be respected, it cannot stand in the way of new development. The preservationists' view is that the city's future lies in its past—as well as with new construction.

Even within the preservation community, however, there has been debate as to whether historic values supersede all other values or whether they constitute only one among many objectives, each of which must compromise. For instance, the Charleston, South Carolina, local preservation community was split over the Charleston Center, a UDAG project. Some, such as Anna Wells Rutledge, a grande dame of Charleston's preservation community, opposed the center entirely, claiming "It will make this place a Coney Island." Others were willing to support it in a modified form more amenable to historic sensitivities:

> Eleanor Hart, who recalls that the Preservation Society started in her mother's ballroom back in 1920, says "Charleston Center is three-quarters good and that's as good as you're going to get." Looking around her own 250-year-old house, she muses, "The Captain and I made some mistakes in restoring this place . . . but it's three-quarters good . . . and nothing's perfect."[29]

The literature tends to simplify preservation's association with neighborhood revitalization. Designation is cast as an independent variable influencing numerous neighborhood-dependent variables, such as an influx of middle-class residents, an increase in the volume of housing rehabilitation, and a jump in property value appreciation. But in reality, the cause-and-effect equation is much more complex; the above-mentioned social, economic, and housing variables both precede and follow designation, and, in fact, they sometimes influence the decision to designate an area as historic.

Thus designation is a dependent variable, influenced by shifting local conditions; in itself, historic preservation will often have little capacity to foster stabilization of impacted inner-city areas.

The Mount Morris Park historic district, in danger of abandonment in the late 1970s, is a case in point. Located in Harlem, it was subject to all the economic and social pressures of an inner-city neighborhood. Arrayed against these forces, historic designation fought a rearguard action. But times change, and the Manhattan real estate market began to flourish. The quest for affordable housing pushed renovation into once-verboten areas, including some portions of Harlem. The Mount Morris

Park historic district is now experiencing some revitalization, or at least stabilization—more so than surrounding locations. Thus, while initially the historic designation of Mount Morris Park could not prevail against the forces of decline, in a more salubrious period, designation is fostering revitalization. Still, revitalization might have occurred anyway.

In sum, the relationship between historic preservation and urban revitalization is complex and evolving. A major concern is that growth and new development—critical to a city's economic vigor—be accommodated while preserving the past.

Displacement

When a neighborhood undergoes revitalization, its less-affluent residents, who cannot afford the rising rents, increasing property taxes, and other charges, may be displaced. As revitalization is often accompanied, if not engendered by, historic preservation, a linkage between historic preservation and displacement is suggested. Numerous studies show that historic neighborhoods undergoing revitalization experience rapid, and often significant, socioeconomic changes. For instance, in 1983, Michael Schill and Richard Nathan examined 1950-70 census data on the socioeconomic profiles of those living in Society Hill in Philadelphia and Georgetown in Washington, D.C.[30] In both cases, the racial complexion changed from a mix of white and nonwhite to almost lily-white; the median family income increased dramatically; the percentage of owner-occupied units rose significantly at the expense of the rental stock; median house values showed a hefty appreciation; and other major shifts occurred, such as a flip in occupational profile from blue collar to managerial-professional, with increases in area residents' educational attainment. The implication is that, as these historic neighborhoods became fashionable, many of the original poorer, nonwhite, less-educated, or elderly residents left, or were forced to leave. A similar pattern is evident in other historic areas undergoing revitalization: Michael Cohen discovered such shifts in Old Towne, Pullman, Sheffield, and other historic neighborhoods in Chicago, and John O'Loughlin and Douglas Munski found the same in New Orleans.[31]

Some studies specifically point to forced movements in historic areas. In 1981, Tim Barnekov and John Caron of the University of Delaware examined social change in the Quaker

Hill district of Newark, Delaware. In a follow-up survey one year later, they found that 20 percent of the residents they had interviewed were no longer there and that many had moved involuntarily because of rising rents, conversion of rental units into condominiums, the combining of several smaller apartments into few larger ones, and the like. Barnekov and Caron, however, view the out-movement as a function of general revitalization in Wilmington and as incidental Quaker Hill's being a historical district.[32]

The more recent national survey also points to numerous instances of displacement occurring in areas designated as historic. About one-quarter of the local preservation commissions found that preservation had displaced many residents; an additional one-half spoke of a less severe, but still noticeable, effect. The ambivalence with which the less advantaged view historic preservation—in part because of displacement—was also revealed by the survey: about 40 percent of the local preservation commissions thought their activities were viewed positively by minority groups; a similar share said the minority reaction was neutral; the remainder (about 20 percent) indicated a negative response. In comparison to the perceived reactions of other groups—property owners, developers, and other city agencies, for example—the minority reaction was the coolest to historic preservation, albeit still favorable.

While displacement is an unwelcome event, it is not always catastrophic. According to a recent Princeton University study, with findings similar to those of others, displacement "did not appear to cause significant hardship among those forced to move":

> . . . only 16 percent indicated that their current home was worse than the one lived in before they were displaced. Sixty-seven percent of the displaced households reported that their housing actually improved. When asked to compare their old and current neighborhoods, 56 percent of the displaced households rated the new neighborhoods better than the old. . . . The number of persons per room remained constant for displaced households.[33]

Further, the disadvantages of displacement are somewhat compensated by gains in other directions. Residents who can afford to stay benefit from property value appreciation and other advantages of a neighborhood on the upswing. The recent national survey showed that, while preservation displaced some residents in historic neighborhoods, in its absence many more would have moved as neighborhood conditions deteriorated. Still, historic areas are not magnets in a back-to-the-city vanguard.[34] Most studies in this area indicate there has been little back-to-the-city movement in terms of returning suburban dwellers.[35] The city also benefits from neighborhood revitalization, as the very changes that encourage some residents to move—increased rents, increased property values, rental-to-condo conversion—work to enhance the community's fisc.[36]

It should also be kept in mind that displacement is not an inevitable result of historic preservation. For instance, low-cost home purchase and/or rehabilitation monies could be made available to lower-income residents of gentrifying neighborhoods to allow these individuals to remain. Rent subsidies also could be provided from federal housing subsidy, community development block grant, and other sources. Such assistance, however, usually is not forthcoming. Thus, while displacement is not an inevitable or direct result of preservation, if not confronted it is a by-product and a significant social cost.

Cost Considerations

Most studies suggest that rehabilitation of the existing built environment is less costly than comparable new construction. A decade ago, I examined over a dozen housing projects in both the public and private sectors for the National Housing Policy Review Task Force of the U.S. Department of Housing and Urban Development, and observed that, while rehabilitation versus new construction costs fluctuated considerably, renovation was usually 10 to 20 percent less expensive.[37]

Studies conducted in the past ten years affirm rehabilitation's frequent cost advantage. A 1976 study of downtown office space indicated over a $70-per-square-foot new construction outlay compared with $40 per square foot for major renovation.[38] While the renovation entailed greater expenses for certain items, such as property acquisition, these were more than offset by economies in hard construction costs, the financing of these outlays, and the like. A 1976 study of thirty rehabilitation projects also pointed to the economies of reusing existing built resources.[39] A 1982 analysis of the Department of Housing and Urban Development's multifamily housing programs provides additional evidence of rehabilitation's economic attractiveness.[40] While federally subsidized new housing units cost $38 to $40 per square foot, rehabilitated housing units were delivered at a cost of $30 to $35 per square foot—a savings of roughly 10 to 20 percent.

But comparing the dollars and cents of rehabilitation with new construction is akin to comparing the proverbial "apples with oranges." Rehabilitation is *not* the same as new construction. Amenities differ, as does the nature of the space provided. At times, and depending on needs, rehabilitation may or may not be superior to new construction. There are also numerous unknowns, such as the expected life of new versus rehabilitated space. If new construction lasts longer, then the initial delivery price advantage of rehabilitation may be offset; if rehabilitation is more durable, then its delivery price advantage is further enhanced. Another "unknown" is operating costs. There is no conclusive data either to confirm or deny the allegation that rehabilitated space is significantly less costly in terms of energy costs, property taxes, maintenance outlays, and so on.

Thus, while the weight of the evidence clearly supports rehabilitation's cost efficiency relative to new construction, the comparison is not a simple one, and there are economic tradeoffs in choosing one versus the other.

Conclusion

There is little question that preservation's effects are mixed. On the positive side are the cost-saving advantages of rehabilitation versus new construction, the encouragement of neighborhood revitalization, economic activity, increased property values, and a fostering of a sense of history, continuity, collective identity, and the like.

But preservation's benefits are realized at a price. When a neighborhood undergoes revitalization, those standing in the way of, or unable to come aboard, the forceful locomotive of property value and rental increases, or rental-to-condo conversions, are forced to move. In regulating alterations and demolitions, preservation may impede the revitalization offered by building anew. Designation restrictions also may limit the options available to owners of historic properties and, in the case of economically improved buildings, can diminish the value of their holdings. Many of these consequences may also result from other land-use controls such as zoning; similarly, other city revitalization strategies have mixed consequences.

While preservation's increased public presence contributes to much applauded rehabilitation and desired neighborhood revitalization, the resulting expanded regulation and displacement are unwelcome by many. At issue is how to maximize preservation's many significant benefits while mitigating unwelcome effects.

— 4 —

Options

The definition of "historic" resources, once confined to "great moments of history," today encompasses many survivors of the past with some call for remembrance. The threshold has also changed from the most significant, beautiful, and/or nostalgic to less demanding tests. With these changes has come a rising tide of "historic" objects. Entries on the National Register of Historic Places and local equivalents have mushroomed in only a few short years. More than numbers have changed. In years past, items would be identified/designated on an individual basis; today it is often en masse, whole neighborhoods or on an even larger scale.[1]

Much of this change is welcome. Preservation should not be confined to the "Mount Vernons." Neighborhoods as entities can be important. And there is nothing inherently wrong with a rising volume of designation, particularly when measured against the loss to the historic inventory that has and continues to occur.

But while the breadth of the current definition of "historic" adds a welcome richness to the endeavor, it carries with it certain perils. The growing frequency of its assignment reduces the concept's significance and calls on conscience for protective action. It is akin to crying "wolf" too often. Breadth also means spreading already limited financial resources thinner. Society may be better off with a smaller inventory of items declared historic that is better cared for than with a greater number afforded little restoration or even protection. Breadth also invites abuse. If an argument can be made for almost anything having historic merit, then the banner of preservation will be fallaciously seized by protagonists in land-use, community development, and housing issues. For Community Development Block Grant (CDBG) monies, the claim may be made that the intended beneficiary neighborhood is historic. While such contentions may not be groundless, a broad definition of "historic" makes them overused and the argument of last resort.

A Tiered Approach

Preservationists must find a way to maintain an intellectually rich sense of the historic without unduly broadening the term and its application so as to detract from it. One means of doing this is through a tiered system of historic classification with different protections accorded to each.[2] Numerous European countries adhere to a tiered approach. In Great Britain, after a survey of historic resources has been conducted by the Ministry's Investigation of Historic Buildings, a provisional list of entries for the national register, divided into three grades, is issued: Grade I contains buildings of outstanding interest; Grade II encompasses buildings of special interest (particularly noteworthy entries are awarded an asterisk—Grade II*); Grade III includes buildings not normally qualifying for the national listing but "important enough to be drawn to the attention of local authorities and others so that the case for preserving them can be fully considered."[3] When entries are approved in statutory form, the grades are dropped.

France maintains two major categories of historic resources: "monuments classes" (the main inventory), which are considered nationally significant, and "monuments inscrits" (the supplemental inventory), which are viewed as not as important, but still worthy of preservation.[4] Different protections are accorded. Demolition is prohibited in "monuments classes"; if this results in a financial burden to the owner (e.g., where the owner has permission to construct a new building), then the national government provides an indemnity. In contrast, demolition is delayed but not prohibited on "monuments inscrits," and financial compensation is unavailable.

There are fundamental differences in the way in which Europe and the United States control land use. Public land-use ownership and regulation are much more prominent abroad than in the United States. But even while acknowledging this distinction, the European strategy of tiering historic resources deserves consideration in this country.

There have been some steps toward a classified historic designation approach in the United States. At the federal level, the National Historic Landmarks (NHL) program includes only those historic resources considered significant to the nation as a whole.[5] While the (roughly 1,600) NHLs are prized as more distinctive than the typical National Register entries (which number about 37,000), they are afforded little extra protection. The National Park Service is directed to maintain closer contact with NHL owners, but limited resources reduce application of the charge. Section 110(f) of the National Historic Preservation Act mandates that NHLs be accorded special protection from federal agency action, in addition to the Section 106 process, but Section 110(f) affords only limited safeguards.

At the local level, a number of communities have opted for classified historic designation. Dallas, Texas, for example, has two categories of landmarks.[6] San Francisco, California, has a multiple-tiered classification approach: buildings with the "highest architectural and environmental importance whose demolition would constitute an irreplaceable loss to the quality and character of downtown" are classified as "significant buildings."[7] A local survey, conducted in 1983, identified 266 such structures and further broke them down into Categories I and II, depending on their level of excellence. The next highest classification is termed "contributory buildings," defined as "contributing to the quality and character of downtown." The "contributory" group, which, according to the survey, consisted of 219 buildings, is also broken down into two subgroups, Categories III and IV, depending on importance. San Francisco's tiered classification serves as the basis for differing levels of public protection. The severest restrictions against demolition and alterations are directed at "Category I—Significant" buildings, the least toward "Category IV—Contributory" structures.

A tiered classification system of historic resources deserves broader consideration in this country. Historic resources do vary in their significance, and this difference should be acknowledged. Adopting some of the terminology used in San Francisco's classification system, the highest classification for historic resources might be termed "significant." A middle-level classification might consist of items considered "important." The lowest threshold would encompass resources viewed as "contributory." The exact terminology and number of categories are not important; the concept of differentiation is.

Protection and incentives should be targeted according to classification, with the greatest effort directed toward the most significant categories. For instance, the local preservation commission might have only an advisory role with respect to "contributory" historic resources; the power to delay demolition of those resources considered "important"; and more stringent control over "significant" buildings. The criteria of "appropriateness" for making alterations would be the highest for the "significant" inventory, which also, unlike the others, would be subject to an affirmative maintenance obligation. These "significant" properties would also be subject to detailed individual monitoring, preferably handled by a preservation agency, since a planning department, charged with the responsibility for the entire city, is not equipped to offer such detailed care. It is less compelling that the preservation agency be given line responsibility for the "important" and "contributory" groups, though the agency could perform an important oversight role.

Federal and state protection and incentives should also differentiate between the "significant," "important," and "contributory" categories. The federal government might impose a Section 4(f) or 110(f) level of planning when government agency actions threaten resources in the "significant" group. The lesser Section 106 review might prevail for the "important" category; none at all for the "contributory" historic resources. A parallel approach to environmental impact statements might be taken: government action that would affect the "significant" inventory would warrant elaborate documentation and discussion of alternatives; the lesser categories would compel more modest treatment. On the state level, "mini"-Section 106 and National Environmental Policy Act requirements might follow along the same lines.

Similar distinctions could be made concerning financial aid. On the local level, "significant" buildings would warrant the fullest range of property tax support—assessment taking into account designation restrictions, abatement following rehabilitation, and tax relief in the case of hardship. "Important" and "contributory" buildings would qualify for only some of these measures (e.g., assessment at true value). A similar gradation would apply to loans and grants. At the federal level, the highest Investment Tax Credit (ITC) might be made available to "significant" properties, lesser percentages to the others. Graded tax policies might also be applied to depreciation. For example, the greatest amount of depreciation potential (more technically, Accelerated Cost Recovery) might be allowed the "significant buildings" by *not* adjusting the depreciable basis of the ITC. On "important" buildings, the depreciable basis might be adjusted by 25 percent of the ITC; for the "contributory" group, the depreciable basis might be adjusted by 50 percent (the current standard).

Opponents of a grading strategy point to numerous conceptual and practical problems. The acknowledged difficulty of defining what is significant is compounded when levels of importance are sought. Even if the process of classifying by grade were simpler, critics of this approach argue that the strategy inevitably condemns to benign neglect those landmarks deemed less important. If only the most significant of the inventory is aided or protected, the remainder will fall by the wayside.

Some argue that instead of distinguishing historic resources on a formal graded basis, differentiation can be accomplished in *planning* for their protection. This concept, which is part of the Resource Protection Planning Process developed by the National Park Service, is commonly referred to as RP3.[8] It moves away from blanket lists and regulation of historic stock to differentiated identification and treatment.

In sum, a tiering strategy is not a novel approach to preservation. It can be effected in various ways—a formal tiering classification such as that adopted by San Francisco and/or differentiation planning such as that embodied by RP3. Either way, tiering's benefits are compelling. One advantage is that it allows for the targeting of limited resources. It also would curtail the abuse of preservation, since the most stringent protections would be available only for the highest classification (the most significant) of historic resources—an imprimatur difficult to obtain on frivolous grounds. Tiering also would do justice to the broad spectrum of items that make up our historic inventory, allowing for the differences in their nature and their need for protection.

The Appropriate Government Role

A fundamental government role is leadership by example. It is incumbent upon government to act in a responsive and supportive fashion toward the historical inventory in its care. Government agencies should identify the historic resources they own or control and should utilize these properties themselves and/or favor private parties willing to preserve such structures. These provisions have been adopted by the federal government in such measures as Executive Order 11593 and the Public Buildings Cooperative Use Act. It is important that they be adhered to. State and local governments should follow suit by promulgating and enforcing similar supportive measures for preservation.

Government also has a role to play with regard to privately owned historic resources. But it should be kept in mind that while such public intervention is legal, it is not necessarily always proper. Public intervention is justified when it serves the public welfare. On this basis, a strong argument can be made for government involvement in preservation when it aids neighborhood revitalization, beautifies the environment, or provides a sense of and link to history, among other benefits. But these threshold tests are not always applied today. And even when public intervention is warranted, there must be sensitivity to its costs—such as the restrictions that designation may impose on property owners. Therefore, any public intervention must proceed with selectivity as well as diligence. With that understood, I would argue that government has a definite role to play in preservation activities.

Standards must be identified by government so as to clearly delineate which items may be designated as historic. While the courts have not demanded a point-by-point specification of criteria for designation, and while they are willing to grant landmark review bodies considerable leeway in interpretation, they have voiced displeasure with current, sometimes vague, designation standards.[9] For example, a United States District Court set aside the designation of land as a National Historic Landmark on grounds that the secretary of the interior had not published "rules of procedure and substantive criteria for qualification."[10] (This oversight was corrected in 1980 amendments to the National Historic Preservation Act.) A Texas court invalidated an Austin preservation ordinance on similar grounds.[11]

Once standards have been defined, government surveys should be undertaken to identify the historic resources that fit the criteria—thus assuring that designation controls are not applied in an ad hoc manner, affecting some property owners but not others in a hit-or-miss fashion. Currently, there are too many cases of shortfalls in this process.

The argument could be made that a comprehensive government survey is legally required. The *Penn Central* case highlighted the issue. In that case, the owners of the terminal charged that the designation of individual properties as landmarks constituted a discriminatory regulation—on the grounds that only selected property owners were singled out for attention and control. But the U.S. Supreme Court held that the landmarking of individual buildings was part of a "comprehensive plan" in which all properties of historic note are under review for possible designation by the Landmarks Preservation Commission.[12] I would argue that a comprehensive survey is a prerequisite to a "comprehensive plan."

The survey is the basis for designation. But before "historic" status is officially imposed, an open hearing should be conducted, at which potentially affected parties must be allowed to present their views. The hearing may be informal (e.g., presentation at a public meeting) or may take the form of a judicial procedure (e.g., it may include cross-examination, expert witnesses, a transcript, etc.). The nature of the process should be guided by the severity of the controls that designation would impose—it should be exacting, for instance, when designation would entail redevelopment restrictions.

The government should also be responsible for establishing—and publishing—standards and guidelines for alterations to landmarked buildings. The secretary of the interior has established such a guide.[13] Much remains to be done, however, especially at the local level. In the absence of standards and guidelines for local districts, property owners and architects will be left guessing as to which rehabilitation is "appropriate." Uncertainty on this issue is particularly troublesome in eclectic historic districts, such as Greenwich Village in New York City, as opposed to those, like the Vieux Carré in New Orleans, with a uniform style.

A relief valve, in the form of a hardship provision, should also be guaranteed by government to property owners adversely affected by designation.[14] The recent national survey of local preservation commissions indicates that this provision is often absent or is only vaguely specified. The first step that must be taken is to establish a uniform definition of "hardship." In New York City, for instance, the threshold is a "reasonable return"—considered to be a "net annual return of 6 percent of the [property's] valuation." This threshold has been criticized as unrealistic, however, in an era of double-digit interest rates. Yet New York City's provision in this regard is much more comprehensive than that found in most other jurisdictions. Whatever the threshold, hardship must be clearly defined before this mechanism can be implemented. Once hardship has been defined, and proved, various forms of relief can be offered by the municipality—property tax reduction or exemption, low-cost rehabilitation loans to reduce operating costs, and so on. If these are inadequate or unavailable, government should consider purchasing the landmark or removing the designation restrictions, which would free the owner to alter or demolish the structure at will.

Some have recommended that government involvement in preservation activities be guided by a comprehensive plan that would specify goals, designation criteria, survey activity, designation measures, the linkage of preservation and city planning, and so on.[15] Such a plan could provide structure to direct local preservation efforts. It could also serve to advise property owners, city agencies, the state historic preservation officer (SHPO), and others of the nature of existing and intended local government preservation activity. While these objectives cannot be faulted, efforts should focus on improving—rather than describing—the government's role in preservation. If a plan could contribute to this end and will not be distracting, then there is merit to its preparation.

Improving Government's Tools

The major federal support for preservation is the Investment Tax Credit (ITC), which has spawned an impressive amount of historic rehabilitation in recent years. Nonetheless, while the ITC is a powerhouse preservation instrument, in many respects it is a narrow one. It is limited to income-producing properties and is governed by "substantial rehabilitation," "75 percent of external wall," and other qualifying tests. Consideration should be given to modifying these strictures where warranted by valid preservation considerations.

More generally, I believe that there is an overemphasis on the tax code as a strategy to provide federal financial aid for preservation. Given the same federal dollar commitment to preservation (see Table 4), there is need for a greater balancing of assistance with other financial vehicles. This, in turn, will permit better planning than is presently available. For example, right now, basic data-gathering and analytical activities are being threatened by diminished grants-in-aid and other funding. This makes for poor preservation, as there are critical gaps in our knowledge. No one knows exactly how many buildings are on the National Register and, more importantly, what their profiles are—that is, type, location, style, relationship to other entries, condition, and so on. On the fiftieth anniversary of the founding of the Historic American Building Survey, only a quarter of the National Park Service's ten thousand historic structures have been documented.[16] Increased financial assistance to the National Historic Preservation Fund, which supports surveying, cataloging, and technical research, would be most beneficial.

A balance of programs also is needed at the local level, as local governments often overemphasize designation at the expense of other preservation tools. While designation is undoubtedly important, it is not adequate unto itself.

This may be illustrated by the fate of several landmark buildings in New York City. For example, in the late 1960s, the Hebrew Immigrant Aid Society (HIAS), the owner of a designated building on the outskirts of Greenwich Village, found that the building no longer served its needs and sought to sell it; the buyer-to-be was a developer, interested in the deal only to obtain the building lot. The Landmarks Preservation Commission—empowered since 1965 to administer designation controls—intervened behind the scenes in an effort to keep the building intact. It contacted Joseph Papp, who saw in the large HIAS structure the makings of an ideal forum for a public theater. Papp purchased the building at a bargain price of $25 per square foot and adaptively reused it.

While Papp proved a savior to the HIAS landmark, the Landmarks Preservation Commission realized that its designation controls would be fighting a rearguard action against the fierce redevelopment forces in New York. Therefore, it sought and secured (in 1968) an amendment to New York City's zoning resolution that granted a transfer-of-development-rights (TDR) option to all city landmarks.[17] This allowed landmark property owners to transfer unused development rights from the landmark site (the sending lot) to other lots. The purchase of the development rights would enable the owner of the receiving lot to increase floor area by an amount up to 20 percent over the governing maximum floor-to-area ratio. The transfer of development rights from the landmark to the receiving lot could occur only between "adjacent" parcels of land—"adjacent" being defined in an expansive manner (e.g., the receiving lot could be physically adjacent to the landmark, or across the street from it, or across an intersection).[18]

Numerous landmark buildings were saved by this mechanism. For instance, there was great pressure to demolish and redevelop the Villard Houses—the former Morgan Mansion, located on one of the prime real estate locations in Manhattan. Relief was found by allowing the property to sell its air rights to an adjacent lot on which the Helmsley Palace Hotel was built. The same forces were at work, albeit in a less dramatic fashion, with reference to a landmark at 311 East 58th Street in Manhattan. The townhouse, containing approximately 2,500 square feet of space, was underdeveloped relative to the intensity of use allowed by zoning (e.g., about 25,000 square feet). The owner of the building, a composer teaching at the Juilliard School of Music, had no interest in moving from his residence; yet the pressure by developers mounted until the future of the landmark was endangered. The matter was resolved when the air rights to the townhouse were sold to permit an apartment house next door.

Then came the Penn Central controversy. While, as of the 1960s, buildings in the Grand Central area had an allowable floor-to-area ratio of 18, Grand Central Terminal used only one-ninth that permitted. This meant that an additional 2.6 million square feet of office and related space could be constructed. To protect against such massive redevelopment, which could destroy the character of Grand Central, the terminal was designated as a landmark. This brought the legal challenge described earlier.

Even while the Landmarks Preservation Commission was defending the designation of the terminal as a historic resource, it was devising a plan to allow Penn Central to capitalize on the unrealized development potential of its property. It again turned to the TDR mechanism for relief. But the requirement of "adjacency" and the 20 percent density-increase ceiling severely limited the applicability of TDR to Grand Central; there were no adjacent lots that could absorb the full 2.6 million square feet of air rights. Consequently, in 1969, the city removed the density-increase ceiling on TDR sales in the central business district and allowed for the transfer of development rights over multiple building lots provided these lots had a common owner (the "chains of title" concept). The removal of the density-increase ceiling worked not only to the advantage of Penn Central but also to that of other owners of landmark properties in the central business district. Allowing "chains of title," on the other hand, was almost exclusively for the benefit of Penn Central, because it owned so many of the nearby properties in the midtown area.

Penn Central eventually sold 75,000 of its 2.6 million square feet of air rights to the Phillip Morris conglomerate, which included these air rights in its corporate headquarters across from Grand Central. Penn Central received $2 million for the air rights, amounting to roughly $30 per square foot. On this basis, Penn Central's remaining air rights have a value of approximately $75 million. It is not clear why Penn Central has not sold off a larger share of its air rights inventory. Possibly the "chain of title" was broken by its sale of numerous midtown properties—including the Biltmore, Roosevelt, Commodore, and Waldorf-Astoria hotels—during the 1970s.

As the above cases show, TDR was a critical local preservation tool in protecting a number of New York City landmark buildings. It clearly merits increased adoption as a preservation mechanism. Yet, according to the recent national survey, only about 10 percent of local preservation commissions allow TDR.

Denver, Colorado, has permitted transfer of development rights from landmarks to contiguous lots since 1980. It subsequently has allowed for districtwide transfers: landmarks in the central business and lower downtown districts can transfer development rights to receiving sites anywhere within their districts.[19] Dallas, Texas, also recently adopted a district TDR mechanism. Owners of landmarks in the city's downtown area can—if they meet specified qualifications—sell unused air rights to others in the same area. (The landmark must be undergoing substantial rehabilitation that will increase the building's value by at least 50 percent, and the increase in floor-to-area ratio of the receiving lots must be within a prescribed limit.)[20] San Francisco also incorporates a TDR mechanism. Development rights can be transferred within any district at a 1:1 ratio from the landmark to the receiving lots. A bonus density increase is accorded if the transfer is to Transbay Terminal—a relatively low-density area in which planners would like to foster new construction in order to relieve the high density of the city's financial core. Wherever the transfers occur, San Francisco also imposes limits on increases in floor-to-area ratio of the receiving lots under prevailing zoning, height, and bulk limits.[21] But these cities are the exception.

While TDR would prove a useful safeguard to historic resources in many more cities than those in which it is currently applied, it should not be mechanically adopted. It is most welcome in instances of stringent designation controls that restrict redevelopment and in cases of underdeveloped landmarks in high-density areas.

In order for the TDR mechanism to be useful, there must be a "demand" for development rights.[22] In communities that allow very high density construction, there is little incentive for developers to purchase additional development credits (one reason why TDR was never adopted in Chicago, for instance—a city permitting very high floor-to-area ratios in its central business district). In such cases, "demand" for TDR credits could be created by downzoning. But the advisability of so drastically changing zoning solely in order to create a TDR market is very questionable. A major change of this sort should be based on general planning considerations, such as utility capacity, transportation system capability, and the like. San Francisco's TDR program accompanied a major downzoning prompted by just such planning concerns.

A marketplace is also necessary to bring together buyers and sellers of development credits. If there is no private mechanism, the city may have to establish a development bank or auction place. (There is some precedent for this where TDR has been applied to conserve critical coastal zone and agricultural areas.) Limiting the range of permitted transfers to adjacent lots severely restricts the usefulness of the TDR mechanism, as it lowers the number of buyers and the value of the credits. While extending the transfer scope would enhance TDR's marketability, it may play havoc with zoning:

> Deciding where the excess density from historic sites will end up surfaced as an important issue pointing to an inherent contradiction between zoning and TDRs. The tension between them becomes particularly acute when there is a "floatation" of rights over a large radius from the building sending them. Presumably, zoning relates to infrastructure, services and other community goals. The problem is how to justify the impacts of additional density over and above what the existing zoning contemplates in an area which is a mile away from the benefit—the preserved historic building.[23]

Thus, while TDR should certainly be considered as an important accompaniment to local designation, there are limitations to its use.

The property tax is another important tool that government can—but rarely does—use to support preservation activities in the public interest. Since property tax is based on property value, it is affected by landmark designation. As discussed earlier, by imposing limitations on the alteration/demolition of a historic building, designation may detract from value by precluding the structure's most profitable use. Conversely, the prestige and other benefits resulting from designation may enhance selling prices. Property value is officially determined by assessors, who should—but typically do not— consider landmark status when making their evaluations.[24]

Failure by assessors to take landmark status into account has serious consequences. If the historic property is assigned an assessment greater than its real worth, then its owner is burdened with an unfairly high obligation. Such overassessment is more than inequitable (as well as illegal), for over time it can contribute to financial pressures discouraging the building's rehabilitation and possibly even essential maintenance. Conversely, if the historic building is undervalued, this underassessment means that the local taxing authority is being denied the fiscal benefit of historic preservation.

Consideration of the problem of assessment inequities is long overdue. A number of states have recently adopted legislation specifying that the assessor must acknowledge the historic status of a property in determining its value for real-taxation purposes.[25] Typical is South Dakota's Statute Section 1-19B-25, which states that the "designation and any recorded restrictions upon the property limiting its use for preservation purposes shall be considered by the assessor for appraising it for tax purposes." Other legislation, such as California's Statute Section 500280-289, requires that properties designated by the federal, state, county, or local government be assessed on the basis of their current, rather than highest and best, use. These measures should be seriously considered for adoption by other states.

The property tax can also be used to "compensate" (in a nonlegal sense) for financial hardship caused by designation. Connecticut authorizes municipalities to abate, in whole or in part, real property taxes on historically or architecturally significant structures if "the current level of taxation is a material factor which threatens the continued existence of the structure."[26] Similarly, in New York City, if the owner of a designated property proves financial hardship, the Landmarks Preservation Commission "is empowered to devise a plan which may include exemption from or reduction of real property taxes." Neither of these measures, however, has been put to use: no Connecticut locality has ever abated property taxes in the instance of landmarks encountering financial stress, and New York City has never approved a property tax remission in cases of hardship.

The property tax can also be administered in such a way as to encourage the rehabilitation of historic buildings. Numerous states, for example, have enacted statutes according favorable property tax treatment to historical buildings undergoing renovation. These provisions range from reducing existing property taxes to not reassessing, or only partially increasing the assessment of, the rehabilitated building. Since rehabilitating the historic property will improve its value and would, under normal circumstances, result in an increased property assessment and tax obligation, these measures convey both relief and incentive.

But while it is an important preservation tool, the property tax is often overlooked. Even in those jurisdictions where there is enabling authority, the property tax provisions are often paper programs only, with little—or no—implementation.[27] Some assessors are not even aware that statutes requiring assessment at current use have been enacted.[28] I would strongly urge that property tax measures in support of historic preservation activities be adopted and activated along the lines of the precedents described above.

Another way in which government could lend support to preservation activities in the public interest would be to adopt building codes that are sensitive to the unique problems inherent in rehabilitation. Currently, standard building codes can be antithetical to the rehabilitation and/or maintenance of historic buildings, as they may impose new building standards on older structures—standards that may be achieved only at tremendous cost. To counter the problem, special building codes should be available for historic buildings. On the state level, California has been a leader in this area. At the national level, a building code proposed by the Building Officials and Code Administrators International (BOCA) incorporates a provision that could serve as a useful model:

> The provisions of this code relating to the construction, repair, alteration, enlargement, restoration and moving of buildings or structures shall not be mandatory for existing buildings or struc-

> tures identified and classified by the state and/or local government authority as historic buildings, subject to the approval of the board of appeals when such buildings are judged by the Building Official to be safe and in the public's interest of health, safety and welfare regarding any proposed construction, alteration, repair, enlargement, relocation, and location within the fire limits. All such approvals must be based on the applicant's complete submission of professional architectural and engineering plans and specifications bearing the professional seal of the designer.[29]

As with property tax measures, however, not only are substantive changes in building code provisions needed, but also action to ensure implementation. Local building code inspectors may be hesitant to accept innovative building code provisions; municipalities must meet this problem head-on through training, education, and firm directives.

Technical assistance is another local government preservation support that should be seriously considered. Financial aid is still another. Municipalities must recognize that some historic buildings are in such severe financial distress that federal investment tax credits alone cannot alleviate the problem. Low-interest rate, revolving-loan programs, and even grant monies may be necessary to ease the strain. These measures can be established from CDBG and other seed money sources. Local tax monies from the burgeoning syndication of ITCs or the tax-increment financing secured by rising property values in historic districts could also be tapped. Cities could also assist in opening conventional financing doors by impressing upon local lenders the positive effects of preservation on property value and neighborhood revitalization. The recommendation that direct or indirect financial aid be made available to historic properties in cases of need is made in full recognition that cities themselves are fiscally hard-pressed. There is, however, no financially painless way to foster the benefits of preservation.

Public financial aid for preservation—whether in the form of tax credits, property tax relief, loans, or grants—must be carefully allocated. Targeting to historic significance is one consideration—the greatest funding to be made available to the most precious historic resources. Targeting to need should also be considered. At the present time, there is little such differentiation. While it is difficult to define the particular circumstances of "need" that deserve public aid, the government had handled this problem in other contexts by imposing cutoff points (e.g., the UDAG eligibility criteria). One way in which a cutoff might be applied is to limit the ITC to applicants demonstrating that "but for" the credit, the proposed rehabilitation would not be feasible.

Some jurisdictions are moving in this direction. For example, New York City's J-51 property tax program, one of the most generous rehabilitation incentives in this country (which has applied to all renovation, not just that of historic buildings), has been reformulated to target public aid for preservation. While J-51 is limited to units whose assessed valuation will remain under $38,000 after redevelopment, this ceiling is lifted in neighborhood preservation districts—nonluxury areas designated by the city as ripe for rehabilitation and requiring assistance to foster such activity.[30]

Government can also aid preservation efforts by acting to counter the displacement problem. A myriad of measures can be applied to limit forced movement or mitigate its adverse effects. For example, in Savannah, Georgia, a group called Savannah Landmarks, which is helping to restore the historic Victorian district (containing an overwhelming number of minorities and poor), has earmarked roughly half of the rehabilitated units for the area's present residents. Financing is coming from a variety of public sources (e.g., CDBG and UDAG monies), as well as from private foundations.[31]

What Savannah Landmarks accomplished in one city, the National Trust for Historic Preservation is fostering on a national basis. To this end, it has formed an Inner-City Ventures Fund (ICVF) that assists neighborhood self-help groups in acquiring houses in historic districts, rehabilitating them, and renting the units to low-income, minority households. The ICVF effort has begun operations in ten to twelve historic neighborhoods across the country; others will be added as funding permits. ICVF hopes to leverage its funding support by securing participation agreements with local lenders and mortgage take-out arrangements with the Federal National Mortgage Association.

These are just two examples of the programs that government could constructively pursue to mitigate one of the costs of historic preservation.

Ensuring Delivery

While administrative problems, such as procedural delays and inadequate enforcement, are not unique to government intervention in preservation activities, these problems are aggravated in this area by severe understaffing. If government is serious about preservation, it cannot continue to make do with the existing catch-as-catch-can personnel commitment, such as staff persons lent by the planning department on an as-available basis.

Another serious problem hindering effective delivery of government support to preservation activities is inadequate linkage on both inter- and intra-governmental levels. While there is a reasonable meshing between federal and state government preservation activities—since the states carry out the provisions of the National Historic Preservation Act (NHPA)—there are discontinuities between the local and other levels of government that must be addressed. For instance, all local communities—not just those certified by the 1980 amendments to NHPA—should participate in National Register proceedings. Certification of local governments (qualifying them for direct financial assistance) should proceed with all due speed. Local governments and states must work together, especially on matters requiring state authorization, such as taxation and building-code regulation.

Inadequate linkage also is a significant concern at the same level of government. At the federal government level, the Department of the Interior, with primary preservation responsibility, and the Department of Housing and Urban Development (HUD), which administers programs of paramount significance to community development in the form of CDBG and UDAG, sit side by side, each engaging in activities of consequence to historic preservation, yet having very little to do with one another. For much of the post-World War II era, HUD programs, such as urban renewal, were antithetical to preservation. Today, the direct confrontation is largely gone, as CDBG and UDAG nominally encourage reuse as opposed to new construction. While latent conflicts with historic preservation occasionally do emerge, for the most part there is neither confrontation nor contact.

Similarly, at the local government level there is often little coordination between the historic preservation and planning processes. Since preservation is tied up with land-use controls, permitting, neighborhood revitalization, and so forth, one idea might be to house responsibility for preservation in the city's planning department. This concept underlies San Francisco's approach to the preservation of historic buildings in its downtown area. It elected to establish conservation districts embodied in the city's land-use plan, as opposed to historic districts administered by a landmark commission, on the following bases:

> (1) with few exceptions, preservation ordinances in other cities have not in themselves been particularly successful in growing downtown areas; (2) the same preservation goals can be accomplished through conservation zones; (3) the trend today in San Francisco is to consolidate the city's power in the planning commission, which makes it politically infeasible to establish an independent landmarks board or commission with regulatory authority; (4) it is wrong, in terms of planning and regulation, to fragment and isolate the decision-making process on historic buildings from the overall planning and regulatory decision-making scheme; and (5) the kind of detailed regulation typically found in historic districts is not appropriate in the downtowns of major cities.[32]

Consolidating preservation, planning, and community development functions in a single department is not easy. Bureaucracies have a life force of their own and, with their service-population allies, resist such radical shifts. There is also a more substantive issue. While planning may encompass preservation, it traditionally has been biased toward new construction. It is also questionable as to whether planners have the experience, expertise, or interest to deal with preservation concerns.[33]

Given these obstacles, rather than consolidation, joint participation in a separate entity might be a superior approach. There is some precedent for this—at both the local and federal levels. For example, about a decade ago, in light of the growing interest in housing rehabilitation, HUD and the Federal Home Loan Bank Board (FHLBB) established the Housing Reinvestment Task Force so that the two departments could bring their respective housing and financial expertise and interests to bear. The task force, which proved most successful, operated for many years throughout the country; its services are now performed by a permanent Neighborhood Reinvestment Corporation.

The Housing Reinvestment Task Force might provide a model for joint participation by HUD and Interior in historic preservation activities, with HUD contributing its housing and community development expertise and Interior its half-century of preservation experience. The intent here is not to expand the federal bureaucratic structure but rather to seek an arm's length vehicle in which HUD and Interior can work together to foster preservation.

Another alternative to consolidation is simply to increase coordination. For example, in a community supportive of preservation, this goal should be incorporated in its comprehensive plan—worked on jointly by the local planning and preservation departments. While strictly the responsibility of the planning department, the local preservation agency might also participate in the drafting of the zoning ordinance, by sharing its firsthand experience with preservation-adverse zoning (e.g., allowing high floor-to-area ratios, bonuses for plazas, etc.) and helping to devise preservation-enhancing zoning provisions such as TDR. Cooperation in working out subdivision ordinances, building codes, and the like would also be constructive. Similarly, while the preservation commission would have primary responsibility for landmark surveys and designation, the planning department should be allowed to comment. Likewise, the review of requests for certificates of appropriateness and for altering or demolishing landmarks, should be open to planning department participation. (The RP3 process, previously described, encourages the integration of preservation planning with other land-use, decision-making mechanisms.)

Increased coordination is also possible at the federal level. For example, the Housing Assistance Plan, now used to target CDBG assistance to areas with low- and moderate-income households, could be used to pinpoint, and indicate the steps needed to protect, the community's historic resources.

In fostering coordination at the federal level, the potential of the Advisory Council on Historic Preservation—which brings together representatives from Interior, HUD, and other federal agencies—should not be overlooked. Much of the Advisory Council's work focuses on the Section 106 process, but it has the potential for more responsibility. Given its multi-agency composition, it can raise awareness about preservation on the federal level, and it can both anticipate and resolve preservation-versus new-development conflicts before the Section 106 process is initiated. The Advisory Council already has attempted these constructive activities; it should be allowed the resources to further foster federal-level preservation coordination.

Private Sector Involvement

Until recently, preservation activity was conducted almost solely by private interests. Despite increasing government involvement, there is room for additional private sector activity.

One of the instruments utilized by the private sector in fostering preservation efforts is historic easements—a "less-than-fee right or interest recorded in the Public Land Record and almost always held in gross by a public agency, charitable trust, or corporation having as one of its purposes the conservation or preservation of environmental or historic resources."[34] Another private sector measure that can be effective in protecting preservation efforts is the restrictive covenant, which can establish architectural controls and prohibit the destruction or alteration of historic properties.[35]

But these private measures have not achieved full acceptance. A major deterrent is the unwillingness of developers, and others, to accept restrictions on their property. This attitude, however, may be changing, partly because of changing social values, partly as the consequence of very generous rehabilitation investment credits. In addition, a tax incentive has been established for historic easements. Section 170(f)(3)(B)(iii) of the Internal Revenue Code provides charitable contribution status for an easement "given in perpetuity for use exclusively for conservation purposes" by a qualifying organization (for example, a private preservation group or a municipal landmarks commission). The charitable contribution, deductible against ordinary income, is equal to the "fair market value of the easement given up" (the difference in property value before and after the easement is established).[36] Another action that could spur easement activity would be to remove common-law restrictions against easements-in-gross (most less-than-fee historic preservation interests are in this form). Many states have already taken such action.

But there are also practical impediments to increased easement activity. One is that an easement can be donated only if there is a receiving body with the resources to enforce the restrictions placed on the use of the property. In many communities, neither government nor appropriate not-for-profit groups are aware of, or are willing to receive, historic easements, thus forestalling the operation of this private preservation mechanism. Clearly, appropriate receiving bodies are a first priority.

Another practical impediment is the determination of the easement's value for tax purposes. While the "before versus after" rule is clear, its application is quite technical. The IRS has challenged numerous easement valuations on the grounds that too much loss was attributed to the easement's creation. It is time for the IRS and the preservation community to work together to facilitate application of the "before versus after" rule.[37]

Another practical problem is that in recently released proposed rules, the IRS required easement donors taking advantage of Section 170(f)(3)(B) to "provide substantial and regular opportunity to view that which is being protected." The basis for this rule is mutuality of benefits—if the public is willing to grant tax concessions to foster preservation easements, it should be able to visually reap the benefit of such protection. The "regular opportunity to view" requirement, however, may discourage easement donations. Similar provisions required for preferred property taxation of landmarked buildings have "scared" many potential users.[38] New Mexico's reduced-assessment provision for the rehabilitation of landmarks has been spurned by many nominally eligible owners because it is available only if significant public access (for twelve days annually) is allowed—a stipulation that in the opinion of the New Mexico SHPO "scares just about everyone." The same is true with respect to California's assessment-at-current-use measure. The benefit of the public-access requirement must be weighed against its potentially inhibiting effect.

Government regulations may also complicate matters. Federal tax law works to encourage the donation of historic easements by according the donor a charitable contribution. (The deduction is equal to the diminished value of the historic resource in that its facade or other portion cannot be altered or demolished as it might in the absence of the easement.) Local designation, on the other hand, can effectively reduce, if not eliminate, the tax incentive for easement donations:

> When an urban historic building is protected by a strong local landmark ordinance, it is difficult for an owner to argue that the donation of an easement takes anything from the bundle of rights that was not given up already as a result of landmark designation. Any decrease in the market value of the property occasioned by demolition or alteration restrictions probably would have occurred at the time of landmark designation. The donation of an easement that merely duplicates protection provided by a landmark ordinance would provide no further effect on value.[39]

Without owner interest, of course, historic easements will fail to promote preservation activity. But even while recognizing the inadequacies of private measures, it is important to allow them to flourish as much as possible, for they offer definite advantages. They can be individually tailored to specific building needs and characteristics, they are less subject to political pressures, they do not raise public-taking issues, and they bring fewer enforcement problems.

A private initiative of a very different sort that would be most beneficial to historic preservation efforts is increased cooperation between the planning and preservation disciplines. Presently, there is little professional recognition. In fact, it was only in 1980 that the American Planning Association "admit[ted] a historic preservation division into its ranks, allowing it to join transportation, environmental protection, and urban design as a legitimate planning function." In 1982, however, the association suspended the group for nonperformance.[40] It is long overdue for the preservation and planning disciplines to recognize each other's legitimacy and work on how best to coordinate their activities. The enthusiasm for historic preservation and the very vigor of the drive demand a more rational and integrated approach.

Notes

Chapter 1

1. Carol M. Rose, "Preservation and Community: New Directions in the Law of Historic Preservation," *Stanford Law Review* 33 (February 1981), p. 476.

2. Tony P. Wrenn and Elizabeth B. Mulloy, *America's Forgotten Architecture* (New York: Pantheon Books, 1976), pp. 18-19.

3. Jacob Morrison, *Historic Preservation Law* (Washington, D.C.: National Trust for Historic Preservation, 1965), p. 1.

4. Cited in Norman Williams, Jr., Edmond H. Kellogg and Frank B. Gilbert, *Readings in Historic Preservation* (New Brunswick, N.J.: Center for Urban Policy Research, 1983), pp. 6-8.

5. Morrison, *Historic Preservation Law,* p. 2.

6. Charles B. Hosmer, *Presence of the Past—A History of the Preservation Movement in the United States before Williamsburg* (New York: G. P. Putnam's Sons, 1965).

7. Wrenn and Mulloy, *America's Forgotten Architecture,* p. 21.

8. John S. Pyke, Jr., *Landmark Preservation* (New York: Citizens Union Research Foundation, 1972), pp. 7-8.

9. Hosmer, *Presence of the Past,* p. 44.

10. Ibid., p. 47.

11. Diane Maddex, ed., *The Brown Book—A Directory of Preservation Information* (Washington, D.C.: Preservation Press, 1983), p. 14.

12. Hosmer, *Presence of the Past,* p. 73.

13. New York State Legislative Committee, 1849.

14. Walter Muir Whitehill, "Promoted to Glory," in *With Heritage So Rich,* U.S. Conference of Mayors (Washington, D.C.: National Trust for Historic Preservation, 1966), p. 142.

15. Constance M. Greiff, *Lost America: From the Atlantic to the Mississippi* (Princeton, N.J.: Pyne Press, 1971), p. 7.

16. Pyke, *Landmark Preservation,* p. 8.

17. "La Recherche du Temps Perdu: Legal Techniques for Preservation of Historic Property," *Virginia Law Review* 55 (1969), p. 305.

18. Christopher J. Duerksen, ed., *A Handbook on Historic*

Preservation Law (Washington, D.C.: Conservation Foundation and the National Center for Preservation Law, 1983), p. 235.

19. 16 U.S.C. sec. 461.

20. U.S. Department of the Interior, National Park Service, *National Park System and Related Areas* (Washington, D.C.: Government Printing Office, 1979).

21. Betsy Chittenden and Jacques Gordon, *Older and Historic Buildings and the Preservation Industry* (Washington, D.C.: National Trust for Historic Preservation, October 1983).

22. U.S. Department of the Interior, National Park Service, *Tax Incentives for Rehabilitating Historic Structures: Facts and Figures 1977-1983* (Washington, D.C.: Government Printing Office, January 1984).

23. Maddex, ed., *The Brown Book*, p. 34.

24. Ibid., p. 35.

25. Pyke, *Landmark Preservation*, p. 1.

26. Advisory Council on Historic Preservation, *The National Historic Preservation Program Today* (Washington, D.C.: U.S. Government Printing Office, 1976). Committee print prepared for the Senate Committee on the Interior and Insular Affairs.

27. Maddex, ed., *The Brown Book*, p. 53.

Chapter 2

1. Abeles and Schwartz Associates et al., "Economic and Legal Mechanisms for Preserving Residential Buildings in Historic Districts" (Unpublished study, October 1979).

2. John M. Fowler, "Historic Preservation and the Law Today," *The Urban Lawyer* 12, no. 1 (Winter 1980), p. 10.

3. David Listokin, Interview with the New York City Landmarks Preservation Commission, February 1984.

4. Abeles and Schwartz Associates, et al., "Economic and Legal Mechanisms for Preserving Residential Buildings in Historic Districts."

5. David Listokin, *Landmarks Preservation and the Property Tax* (New Brunswick, N.J.: Center for Urban Policy Research, 1982).

6. Eugenie Birch and Douglass Roby, "The Planner and Preservationist: An Uneasy Alliance," *Journal of the American Planning Association* 50, no. 2 (Spring 1984), p. 194.

7. U.S. Department of the Interior, Heritage Conservation and Recreation Service, *Sources of Preservation Funding* (Washington, D.C.: U.S. Government Printing Office, 1979), p. 3.

8. Diane Maddex, ed., *The Brown Book—A Directory of Preservation Information* (Washington, D.C.: Preservation Press, 1983).
9. Christopher J. Duerksen, ed., *A Handbook on Historic Preservation Law* (Washington, D.C.: Conservation Foundation and the National Center for Preservation Law, 1983), p. 248.
10. Advisory Council on Historic Preservation, "The Advisory Council on Historic Preservation and the Protection of Cultural Resources—An Outline of the Process Established by Section 106 of the National Historic Preservation Act," 1980.
11. David Listokin, Interview with the Office of Management and Budget, February 1984.
12. Lars A. Hanslin, "Federal Framework for Historic Landmark Protection—1981," in *Historic Preservation Law,* ed. Nicholas A. Robinson (New York: Practicing Law Institute, 1981), p. 42.
13. U.S. Department of the Interior, National Park Service, "Information Update: Tax Incentives for Rehabilitating Historic Buildings" (January 25, 1985), p. 1.
14. Ibid.
15. Advisory Council on Historic Preservation, *Federal Tax Law and Historic Preservation—A Report to the President and the Congress, 1983* (Washington, D.C.: U.S. Government Printing Office, 1983), pp. 22-23.
16. National Trust for Historic Preservation, "Significant State Historic Preservation Statutes," *Information: From the National Trust for Historic Preservation,* Information Sheet no. 21, 1979.
17. Michael Mantell, "Using State Preservation Laws to Protect Landmarks: New Directions," in *Reusing Old Buildings—Preservation Law and the Development Process,* Conservation Foundation et al. (Washington, D.C.: Conservation Foundation, 1983), p. 396.
18. Ibid., p. 399.
19. Michael Mantell, "State Preservation Law," in *A Handbook on Historic Preservation Law,* ed. Christopher J. Duerksen (Washington, D.C.: Conservation Foundation and the National Center for Preservation Law, 1983), p. 159.

Chapter 3

1. Jane Trichter, "Designation? Certainly, How Much? The Debate," *The New York Times,* Sunday, May 24, 1980, p. 8.
2. Daniel Rose, "Designation? Certainly, How Much? The Debate," *The New York Times,* Sunday, May 4, 1980, p. 8.

3. Advisory Council on Historic Preservation, *Report to the President and the Congress of the United States, 1979* (Washington, D.C.: U.S. Government Printing Office, 1979), p. 1.

4. Michael D. Ainslie, "Venturing Into the Inner City," *Preservation News*, vol. 21, no. 5 (May 1981), p. 5.

5. Tony P. Wrenn and Elizabeth B. Mulloy, *America's Forgotten Architecture* (New York: Pantheon Books, 1976).

6. Advisory Council, *The Contribution of Historic Preservation to Urban Revitalization* (Washington, D.C.: U.S. Government Printing Office, 1979), p. 1.

7. Cited in Diane Maddex, *The Brown Book—A Directory of Preservation Information* (Washington, D.C.: Preservation Press, 1983), p. 103. Original citation by Stipe found in *North Carolina Central Law Journal* 11, no. 2 (Spring 1980).

8. Gene Bunnel, ed., *A Future from the Past* (Washington, D.C.: U.S. Department of Housing and Urban Development and Massachusetts Department of Community Affairs, 1978), p. 67.

9. Advisory Council, *Report to the President*, 1979, p. 1.

10. Ralph W. Miner, *Conservation of Historic and Cultural Resources* (Chicago: American Society of Planning Officials, 1969), p. 2.

11. Robert E. Stipe, *Legal Techniques in Historic Preservation* (Washington, D.C.: National Trust for Historic Preservation, 1972), p. 1.

12. Thomas J. Reed, "Land Use Controls in Historic Areas," *Notre Dame Lawyer* 44 (February 1969), p. 385.

13. Cited in Maddex, *The Brown Book*, p. 102. Original citation by Goldberger found in National Trust for Historic Preservation, *Preservation: Toward an Ethic in the 1980s* (Washington, D.C.: Preservation Press, 1980).

14. For a more detailed discussion, see David Listokin, *Landmarks Preservation and the Property Tax* (New Brunswick, N.J.: Center for Urban Policy Research, 1982).

15. Edgar A. Smith, "Grand Central Station—Landmark at the End of the Line, or End of the Line for Landmarks?—New York City's Landmark Law in the Courts," *University of Pittsburgh Law Review* 37 (1975), p. 97; George J. Siedell, "Landmark Preservation after Penn Central," *Real Property Probate and Trust Journal* 17, no. 3 (Summer 1982), p. 342.

16. *Penn Central Transportation Company v. New York City*, 438 U.S. 104, 1978; 98 S.Ct. (1978), 2646, at 2651, 2662.

17. 98 S.Ct. 2646.

18. *San Diego Gas & Electric*, 450 U.S. 621, 101 S.Ct. 1287, 1981.

19. 446 N.E.2d, 95 Illinois 2d, 1983; cited in Richard J. Roddewig, *Preparing an Historic Preservation Ordinance* (Chicago: American Planning Association, 1983), p. 6. Planning Advisory Service Report no. 374.

20. Roddewig, *Preparing an Historic Preservation Ordinance*, p. 6; Gary L. Tygesson, "Allocating the Cost of Historic Preservation: Compensation for the Isolated Landmark Owner," *Northwestern University Law Review* 74, no. 4 (1979), p. 646; David Bonderman, "Constitutional Issues for Preservation Law," *Legal Notes Quarterly* 1 (1980-81), p. 109.

21. Committee on Religious Leaders of the City of New York, *Interfaith Commission to Study the Landmarking of Religious Property* (New York: Interfaith Commission, January 26, 1982).

22. Brendan Gill, "Block St. Bart's Request," *The New York Times*, January 28, 1984, p. 23; Ralph C. Menapace, "Preservation Laws and Houses of Worship," in *Historic Preservation Law*, Nicholas A. Robinson (1982).

23. *Lutheran Church in America v. City of New York*, 35 N.Y. 2d 121, 132, 316, N.E.2d 305, 311-12, 359 N.Y.S.2d 7, 17 (1974).

24. *Society for Ethical Culture v. Spatt*, 51 N.Y.2d 449, 415 N.E.2d 922, 434 N.Y.S.2d 932 (1980).

25. N. J. L'Heureux, "Allowing Building at St. Bart's," *The New York Times*, January 28, 1984, p. 23.

26. Gill, "Block St. Bart's Request."

27. Advisory Council, *Contribution of Historic Preservation*, p. 4.

28. "Final Wylie Amendment—Historic Review Rules for UDAG Published," *Housing and Development Reporter—Current Developments*, August 31, 1981, p. 276.

29. Tom Huth, "Should Charleston Go New South?" *Historic Preservation*, July-August 1979, p. 38.

30. Michael H. Schill and Richard P. Nathan, *Revitalizing American Cities—Neighborhood Reinvestment and Displacement* (Albany: State University of New York Press, 1983).

31. Michael Cohen, "Historic Preservation and Public Policy: The Case of Chicago," *The Urban Interest* 2, no. 2 (Fall 1980), p. 3; John O'Loughlin and Douglas C. Munski, "Housing Rehabilitation in the Inner City: A Comparison of Two Neighborhoods in New Orleans," *Economic Geography* 55 (January 1979), p. 52.

32. David Listokin, interview with John Caron, February 1984.

33. Schill and Nathan, *Revitalizing American Cities*, p. 7.

34. Abeles and Schwartz Associates et al., "Economic and

Legal Mechanisms for Preserving Residential Buildings in Historic Districts" (Unpublished study, October 1979).

35. Franklin J. James, *Back to the City: An Appraisal . . .* (Washington, D.C.: Urban Institute, 1977).

36. Howard Sumka, "Displacement in Revitalizing Neighborhoods," in *Occasional Papers in Housing and Community Affairs*, U.S. Department of Housing and Urban Development (Washington, D.C.: U.S. Government Printing Office, 1978), p. 134.

37. George Sternlieb and David Listokin, "Rehabilitation versus Redevelopment: Cost Benefit Analyses," *Housing in the Seventies—Working Papers*, vol. 2 (Washington, D.C.: U.S. Government Printing Office, 1976).

38. National Trust for Historic Preservation, *Economic Benefits of Preserving Old Buildings* (Washington, D.C.: Preservation Press, 1976), p. 86.

39. Advisory Council on Historic Preservation, *Adaptive Reuse: A Survey of Construction Costs* (Washington, D.C.: U.S. Government Printing Office, 1976).

40. Urban Systems Research and Engineering, Inc., *The Costs of HUD Multifamily Housing Programs* (Washington, D.C.: U.S. Government Printing Office, May 1982).

Chapter 4

1. Christopher J. Duerksen, ed., *A Handbook on Historic Preservation Law* (Washington, D.C.: Conservation Foundation and the National Center for Preservation Law, 1983), p. 40.

2. Advisory Council on Historic Preservation, *The National Historic Preservation Program Today* (Washington, D.C.: U.S. Government Printing Office, 1976), p. 44. Committee print prepared for the U.S. Senate, Committee on Interior and Insular Affairs.

3. Ibid., p. 80.

4. Robert E. Stipe, ed., *Historic Preservation in Foreign Countries* (Washington, D.C.: U.S. National Committee of the International Council on Monuments and Sites, 1982), p. 11.

5. Donald L. Dworsky, "Federal Law," in *A Handbook on Historic Preservation Law*, ed. Duerksen, p. 229.

6. Dallas, Texas, Department of Planning and Development, "Landmark Preservation Incentives," 1984.

7. San Francisco Department of City Planning, *Downtown*, August 1983, p. 63.

8. Basic elements of RP3 include: "(1) the consideration of managerial issues of scale, logistics, and goals; (2) the partition of resource data into units of manageable size which have a unifying cultural concept, and defined time and space limits; (3) the characterization of survey information, property types, and locational patterns, recognition of data gaps, identification of important historic values, and description of the relationships between properties, property types, and historic values; (4) the definition of (ideal) goals for further identification, evaluation, and treatment of historic properties associated with the group; (5) the modification of the goals into an operational plan based on an analysis of the planning environment and assimilation of the operational objectives into the local administrative processes for use in land management decisions; and (6) the incorporation of new information back into the planning process." See Lawrence E. Aten, "Forum on Historic Preservation Planning: The Resource Protection Planning Process," *The Forum*, vol. V, no. 2 (December 1983), p. 2.; Lachlan F. Blair, "Preservation Embraces Comprehensive Planning," *Planning and Public Policy*, vol. 10, no. 2 (August 1984), pp. 1-2.

9. Christopher J. Duerksen, "The Local Regulatory Process," in *Study Materials and Papers Prepared . . .*, Conservation Foundation et al. (1983), pp. 27-28.

10. *Historic Green Springs, Inc. v. Bergland*, 497 F.Supp. 839 (1980).

11. *Southern National Bank of Houston v. City of Austin*, 582 S.W.2d 229 (1979).

12. *Penn Central Transportation Co. v. City of New York*, 98 S.Ct. 2646, 2663-64 (1978).

13. W. Brown Morton III and Gary L. Hume, *The Secretary of the Interior's Standards for Historic Preservation Projects* (Washington, D.C.: Government Printing Office, 1979).

14. Richard J. Roddewig, *Preparing an Historic Preservation Ordinance* (Chicago: American Planning Association, 1983). Planning Advisory Service Report no. 374.

15. Ibid.

16. Advisory Council on Historic Preservation, *Report to the President and the Congress of the United States* (Washington, D.C.: U.S. Government Printing Office, 1983), p. 69.

17. Norman Marcus, "Air Rights Transfers in New York City," *Law and Contemporary Problems* 36 (1971), p. 372.

18. Norman Marcus, "The Grand Slam Grand Central Terminal Decision," *Ecology Law Quarterly* 7 (1978), p. 731.

19. David R. Burch and Stephen M. Ryals, "Land Use Con-

trols: Requiem for Zoning and Other Musings," *The Urban Lawyer* 15, no. 4 (1983), p. 894.

20. Dallas, Texas, Department of Planning and Development, "Landmark Preservation Incentives," 1984.

21. Nancy Shanahan, "Downtown Preservation Strategies and Techniques," p. 3. (Workshop sponsored by the National Trust for Historic Preservation, June 29, 1983).

22. Ibid., p. 5.

23. Ibid., p. 6.

24. David Listokin, *Landmarks Preservation and the Property Tax* (New Brunswick, N.J.: Center for Urban Policy Research, 1982).

25. Ibid.

26. Conn. Gen. Stat. Ann. Section 12-127a.

27. Listokin, *Landmarks Preservation and the Property Tax.*

28. Ibid.

29. BOCA 516.1, 1981; cited in Duerksen, *A Handbook on Historic Preservation Law,* p. 54.

30. *RSA* [Rent Stabilization Association] *Reporter,* November 1983, p. 11.

31. Chester Hartman et al., *Displacement—How to Fight It* (San Francisco: Legal Services Anti-Displacement Project, 1981), p. 164.

32. Shanahan, "Downtown Preservation Strategies and Techniques," p. 8.

33. Ibid.

34. Ross Netherton, "Restrictive Agreements for Historic Preservation," *The Urban Lawyer* 12, no. 1 (Winter 1980), p. 55.

35. Thomas J. Reed, "Land Use Controls in Historic Areas," *Notre Dame Lawyer* 44 (February 1969), p. 381.

36. Richard J. Roddewig and Jared Shlaes, "Appraising the Best Tax Shelter in History," *The Appraisal Journal* 50, no. 1 (January 1982), p. 28.

37. Advisory Council on Historic Preservation, *Federal Tax Law and Historic Preservation;* Roddewig and Shlaes, "Appraising the Best Tax Shelter in History."

38. Listokin, *Landmarks Preservation and the Property Tax.*

39. Roddewig and Shlaes, "Appraising the Best Tax Shelter in History," p. 31.

40. Eugenie Ladner Birch and Douglass Roby, "The Planner and the Preservationist: An Uneasy Alliance," *Journal of the American Planning Association* 50, no. 2 (Spring 1984), p. 194.

Appendix

NATIONAL HISTORIC PRESERVATION SURVEY*
(TELEPHONE)

Date: ________________

State	______________________
Community	______________________
Size	Population (72,500 median) Housing Units (28,000 median)
Contact Person	James J. Nemeth, Rutgers University
Telephone	______________________

I—BACKGROUND

1. When were historic preservation (designation) controls first enacted in this community?

   1974 (median) (range from 1930 to 1984)

2. What is the *legal basis* of these (designation) controls?

0.6%	State constitution
7.6	State-enabling legislation
35.4	Local ordinance
5.7	Zoning authority
0.0	Home rule
3.2	Constitution & local ordinance
34.8	State enabling & local ordinance
12.7	Any other combinations
100.0%	

3. What is the *scope* of these (designation) controls?

28.8%	Areawide (district)
3.8	Individual buildings
67.3	Areawide and individual
100.0%	

* Because of rounding, the indicated totals may not equal 100.0%.

4. Approximately how many *structures* are *subject to preservation* (designation) controls?

a. *Today:* 184 (median) 798 (mean)

b. Projected number of structures subject to controls a *decade* from now:
300 (median) 1050 (mean)

5. What body/agency *administers* these (designation) controls?

57.1%	Separate landmarks commission
9.0	City planning department
4.5	Other city agency
0.6	Legislative body
1.9	Other (specify)
24.4	Landmarks commission and any other combination
2.6	Any other combination besides above
100.0%	

5a. If landmarks commission administers controls, how many members does it contain?
7 (median)

5b. Must commission members have the following professional expertise?

7.9%	Architecture
0.0	Attorney
1.6	Art historian
10.3	Other
18.9	Any combination of 2 of the above
57.5	Any combination of 3 or more of the above
3.9	None
100.0%	

5c. Do you have a *paid* staff?

50.0%	Yes
50.0	No
100.0%	

5d. If yes, how many *full-time* members (or equivalent)?

one to two (median)

6. Is there any form of an overall historic preservation *plan* (encompassing a comprehensive preservation approach as opposed to designation controls only)?

41.4%	Yes
51.6	No
7.0	Other (specify)
100.0%	

7. Is this plan and/or the local historic preservation activity *linked to* or *coordinated with* the community's:

a. Comprehensive plan?

56.2%	Yes
41.5	No
2.3	Other
100.0%	

Describe ______________________________

b. Zoning ordinance?

46.6%	Yes
51.1	No
2.3	Other
100.0%	

Describe ______________________________

c. Subdivision ordinance?

29.7%	Yes
70.2	No
0.0	Other
100.0%	

Describe ______________________________

d. Building code?

31.4%	Yes
66.2	No
2.4	Other
100.0%	

Describe ______________________________

e. Other regulations? (e.g., Environmental Impact Statements)

44.4%	Yes
53.5	No
2.0	Other
100.0%	

Describe ______________________

II—HISTORIC PRESERVATION ACTIVITIES/POWERS

8. Criteria for/designation of historic buildings/districts:

What are the *criteria* for historic designation?

a. *Age* qualification:

10.1%	Yes, over 30 years
50.3	Yes, over 50 years
10.7	Yes, other
28.9	No
100.0%	

b. Other *criteria*:

6.6%	Architectural
5.3	Historical
1.3	Aesthetic
3.3	Other
18.5	Any combination of 2 of the above
64.9	Any combination of 3 or more of the above
100.0%	

c. Is there a formal *inventory/survey* of historic buildings/districts?

89.2%	Presently
5.7	In planning
0.0	Hoped for
5.1	No
100.0%	

d. *Who* will/who has *conduct(ed)* this survey?

32.2%	Consultants
24.7	City
25.3	Historical society
17.8	Other
100.0%	

If a survey has been (will be) conducted, how *comprehensive* is it (will it be)?

e. *Area*

54.0%	Citywide
43.3	Selected areas
2.7	Other
100.0%	

f. *Type*

3.9%	Residential only
2.6	Commercial only
93.5	Residential & commercial
100.0%	

g. Will/has the survey be(en) *updated*?

56.3%	Yes
37.3	No
6.3	Other
100.0%	

9. Describe the *process* of historic designation.

a. Process (brief, in flow-chart outline):

56.4%	Legislative approval
43.6	No legislative approval
100.0%	

b. Is property owner *consent/initiation* necessary?

49.3%	Yes
49.3	No
1.4	Other
100.0%	

c. Is designation considered as a *legislative* or *adjudicative* (judicial) process—the latter requiring *procedural due process* (a judicial-like proceeding—requiring transcripts, right of cross-examination, etc.)?

75.5%	Legislative process
14.4	Adjudicative process
10.1	Other
100.0%	

d. Do these *present processes* represent a *change* from past procedures? How?

18.1%	Yes
81.8	No
0.1	Other
100.0%	

10. Designation *scope*?

19.1%	Facade (visible from street)
55.3	Entire exterior
0.0	Interior only
25.7	Exterior and interior
100.0%	

The following questions are posed to define the *jurisdiction* of the local historic commission (or equivalent body). What *activities* does it regulate (e.g., demolition, alterations, etc.) as well as the *level* of control or *powers* it exerts (advisory only, delay demolition/alterations, etc.)?

11. *Historic Commission* Jurisdiction

a. Demolition

97.4%	Yes
2.6	No
100.0%	

b. Moving (building)

89.9%	Yes
10.1	No
100.0%	

c. Alterations

98.1%	Yes
1.9	No
100.0%	

d. New Construction

93.5%	Yes
5.9	No
99.4%	

12. *Historic Commission Powers*

a. Demolition

13.8%	Advisory
32.9	Delay
53.3	Final, with appeal to ____
100.0%	

b. Moving (building)

17.5%	Advisory
16.8	Delay
65.7	Final, with appeal to ____
100.0%	

c. Alterations

15.8%	Advisory
9.9	Delay
74.3	Final, with appeal to ____
100.0%	

d. New Construction

15.2%	Advisory
9.7	Delay
75.2	Final, with appeal to ____
100.1%	

e. Earthmoving

62.5%	Yes
37.5	No
100.0%	

e. Earthmoving

17.1%	Advisory
13.2	Delay
69.7	Final, with appeal to ____
100.0%	

13. How are the historic preservation controls described above *enforced*?

1.3%	Windshield survey
3.9	On-site cyclical inspection
25.7	Notification by building/other city department
0.0	Block/other group monitoring
1.3	Public complaints
0.7	Answers 2 and 3 above
13.8	Any other combination of 2 items above
53.3	Combinations of 3 or more
100.0%	

13a. Is a "certificate of appropriateness" (C of A) or equivalent utilized for effectuating regulations?

82.4%	Yes
15.0	No
2.7	Other
100.0%	

13b. What constitutes a building "alteration" for which a "C of A" must be applied for?

58.6%	All work done on property
40.6	Only work requiring a building permit
0.8	Other
100.0%	

14. What are the *penalties* for violating preservation controls?

a. *Penalties?*		b. Are they typically applied?			
32.8%	Fines	22.6%	Yes	77.4%	No
4.0	Injunction	33.9	Yes	66.1	No
4.0	Replacement	25.6	Yes	74.4	No
1.6	Other	15.8	Yes	84.2	No
3.2	Fines and injunction				
28.0	Any other combination of 2 of the above				
26.4	Any combination of 3 or more				
100.0%					

15a. Do owners of historic buildings have an *affirmative maintenance obligation*?

28.9%	Yes
70.4	No
0.7	Other
100.0%	

15b. What does this consist of?

15c. Is it enforced?

63.5%	Yes
36.5	No
100.0%	

16a. Does the historic preservation ordinance contain a *hardship provision*?

40.1%	Yes
59.2	No
0.7	Other
100.0%	

16b. *Provisions?*

12.5%	Rate of return
81.3	"Excessive" costs (unspecified)
6.3	Other
100.0%	

16c. Are the *provisions the same* for all parties (private, tax-exempt, etc.)?

88.1%	Yes
11.9	No
100.0%	

16d. Has the hardship provision been *used*?

39.0%	Yes
59.3	No
1.7	Other
100.0%	

17. Are owners of historic buildings offered the following *economic/technical assistance*:

a. Transfer of development rights?

10.0%	Yes
89.3	No
0.7	Other
100.0%	

b. Property tax relief?

29.1%	Yes
69.5	No
1.3	Other
100.0%	

c. Subsidized loans/grants?

64.5%	Yes
33.6	No
2.0	Other
100.0%	

d. Assistance in securing private loans?

27.9%	Yes
71.4	No
0.6	Other
100.0%	

e. Technical assistance?

84.6%	Yes
14.7	No
0.6	Other
100.0%	

f. Other aid?

32.3%	Yes
65.4	No
2.4	Other
100.0%	

18. Are *church-owned properties* treated any differently with respect to:

a. Designation?

4.1%	Yes
95.2	No
0.7	Other
100.0%	

b. Hardship?

1.5%	Yes
98.5	No
100.0%	

c. Economic/other assistance?

2.9%	Yes
95.7	No
1.4	Other
100.0%	

d. Other? (describe)

5.3%	Yes
94.0	No
0.8	Other
100.0%	

III—OTHER IMPACTS/FUTURE

19. What has been the *reaction* to historic preservation controls by:

a. Property owners of designated buildings?

28.0%	Strongly positive
41.2	Positive
22.4	Neutral
6.5	Negative
2.0	Strongly negative
100.0%	

b. Developers?

16.7%	Strongly positive
41.0	Positive
19.4	Neutral
16.7	Negative
6.3	Strongly negative
100.0%	

c. Other city agencies?

16.4%	Strongly positive
55.3	Positive
23.0	Neutral
3.3	Negative
2.0	Strongly negative
100.0%	

d. Municipal legislature?

24.5%	Strongly positive
55.0	Positive
15.2	Neutral
4.6	Negative
0.7	Strongly negative
100.0%	

e. Minority groups?

7.5%	Strongly positive
35.8	Positive
40.8	Neutral
15.0	Negative
0.8	Strongly negative
100.0%	

f. Newspapers?

24.8%	Strongly positive
57.7	Positive
15.3	Neutral
1.5	Negative
0.7	Strongly negative
100.0%	

20. What has been preservation's *social impact* on:

a. Neighborhood group formation?

65.5%	Encouraged formation
34.5	No impact
100.0%	

b. Gentrification?

23.2%	Has displaced many existing residents
43.8	Has displaced few existing residents
33.0	Has encouraged existing residents to stay
100.0%	

21. What has been preservation's *economic impact* on:

a. Rehabilitation volume? (of designated properties)

49.3%	Substantial increase
34.7	Moderate increase
16.0	No change
0.0	Negative impact
100.0%	

b. Property values? (of designated buildings)

50.3%	Substantial increase
34.5	Moderate increase
15.2	No change
0.0	Negative impact
100.0%	

c. Tourism? (in designated areas)

32.2%	Substantial increase
34.3	Moderate increase
33.6	No change
0.0	Negative impact
100.0%	

d. Retail sales? (in designated areas)

23.6%	Substantial increase
31.4	Moderate increase
43.6	No change
1.4	Negative impact
100.0%	

22. Are *federal tax credits* for historic rehabilitation:

a. Being used? (approximate volume—number of structures)

76.8%	Under 50
9.8	50-100
4.5	100-200
7.1	200-500
1.8	500$
100.0%	

b. How can the usefulness of tax credits be improved?

faster processing; local approval; allow for owner-occupied units

23. What has been the *regulatory impact* of the public preservation controls?

a. From time of application, how long does it usually take to receive a certificate of appropriateness?

61.5%	Under one month
33.8	1-3 months
1.5	4-6 months
3.1	Over 6 months
100.0%	

b. What share (%) of the applications for these certificates are approved?

0.0%	0-25%
0.0	25-50%
1.7	50-75%
16.0	75-90%
82.4	Over 90%
100.0%	

c. How can the regulatory process be expedited or in other ways improved?

Publish standards; expand staff; pre-application conferences

24. Are *private historic preservation controls* allowed/encouraged?

a. Restrictive covenants

50.8%	Yes
49.2	No
100.0%	

b. Easements

52.8%	Yes
47.2	No
100.0%	

c. Are there legal impediments to the application of private preservation controls?

9.3%	Yes
90.7	No
100.0%	

25. What do you think is the proper relationship between *private* and *public* preservation controls?

54.5%	Cooperative public and private controls
25.8	Greater emphasis on private
19.7	Greater emphasis on public
100.0%	

26. What *changes would you recommend* with reference to historic preservation controls and/or implementation? Federal? State? Local?

Improve administration; increase funding; clarify standards

27. How do you envision historic preservation in the United States a *decade* from now:

a. Scale of designation—increasing? decreasing?

86.9%	Increase
4.6	Decrease
8.5	About the same
100.0%	

b. Legal dimension?

55.7%	More stringent controls
25.7	Less stringent controls
18.6	Other
100.0%	

c. Social dimension?

Develop greater preservation consciousness; address gentrification

d. Economic dimension?

Foster rehabilitation; enhance property values